...in Brilliant
...rease Your Personal and Professional Profit

...nyK® International Publishing
...inted in the United States of America

ISBN   0-9724709-0-5 Hardcover

Disclaimer
This book is intended to provide an uplifting means to increase the potential of your brain. It is not intended to replace the care of your doctor(s), psychiatrist, nutritionist or any other professional caregiver.

Attention Schools and Businesses
Brain Brilliant books are available at quantity discounts with bulk purchase for educational, business or sales promotional use. For information regarding bulk purchases, please write to:

AmyK International
Special Sales Department
PO Box 421276
Atlanta, Georgia 30342

www.AmyKInternational.com

D1489232

Brain Brilliant

Increase Your Personal and Professional Profit

AmyK Hutchens

**Every perception, thought, feeling, decision and a
its own neural circuitry. Through the understandin
your mind works you can literally change you
circuitry and change your life.**

AmyK International Publishing
Atlanta

to my parents
Philip and Kathleen
two incredibly Brain Brilliant minds
for their never ending
support, encouragement and love

and

to
Mark, Karen, Lauren and Kristen
and
Bryan, Heather and Robert
an exceptionally fun-loving and wonderful family

Table of Contents

Acknowledgments

Be Brain Brilliant, Increase Your Personal and Professional Profit did not reach your hands and mind without the help of many people. First, I want to thank all of the doctors, scientists, researchers, educators and individuals who study the brain every day of their lives to better understand its inner workings. Their efforts have provided the gift of a healthier life to many.

I would like to specifically convey a heartfelt thank you to Marian, for her wisdom, sense of humor and entrepreneurial camaraderie; to Shannon, for her enthusiasm, passion, belief and dedication to a vision; to Jim and Marie for many a hysterical evening of cranium expansion; and to Shary, for listening (a lot!), for her words of encouragement and for her amazing insight, honest feedback and incredible friendship.

I would also like to express a very special thank you to Brian for his faith in me throughout this whole process. He wields an editor's pen like a sword, and he accepts and respects my brain in all its wonder and wackiness. He is the ideal friend. All of these people are extraordinarily brain brilliant and extraordinarily appreciated.

Introduction
Who are you?

Before you respond by stating your given name, or your status in relation to another, or with the italicized title on your business card, answer this... "What's going on in your mind?"

If you can answer it, you are one step closer to knowing who you really are. Who you really are is not your given name, your nickname nor the roles you play. Who you are, is in part, the sum of a lifetime of experiences that your brain has perceived, processed, organized, filed and stored. You are your brain and the genes, cells, experiences, perceptions, associations and neural pathways in it.

Every perception, feeling and thought you have, every decision you make, and every action you take has its own neural circuitry. Through the understanding of how your mind works you have the possibility to literally change your neural circuitry and change your behaviors. Thus, changing how you might answer the question above and how you might change your life.

Hundreds of books have been written about motivating yourself, increasing your skill sets, making changes, handling stress, acquiring more money and getting the girl or guy in the process if you're lucky.

Many of these books essentially ignore your brain. They espouse theories for improving your life without granting any consideration to the brain. The majority of us completely ignore our brain until it throbs with the dull pain of a headache, whereupon we take two aspirin and tolerate the mild annoyance until we can go back to life as usual. Unfortunately, this "deal-with-it-only-if-it's-irritating-me" mentality is stifling if you are seeking to make serious strides in your personal and professional development.

For example:
Have you ever told another to "Stay calm!" only to discover when it was too late that these words just made them madder?

Have you ever been in an argument and not until it was over did you think of exactly what you should have said, but didn't?

Have you ever put your foot in your mouth and when you tried to remove it you only ended up inserting it further?

Have you ever balked at the idea of change, but days later found yourself actually liking the new way ten times better than the old way?

Have you ever analyzed all your options, made the "best" decision possible, and yet, were still left feeling disillusioned with the results of your choices?

To fully comprehend why these types of things happen in your life you need to know about and understand the machine that determines your perceptions and behaviors in the first place.

Popular opinion has supported the idea that happiness, the key to life, the best-kept secret, etcetera is to know yourself. This concept is found across religions, races, cultures, ideologies and continents. To know yourself, to truly discover the best of who you are, the strengths upon which to build, the weaknesses in which to improve, the potential you possess to realize your individual and unique greatness is to learn about the machine that drives your reason, your decisions, your actions, your imagination and your passions; the machine that drives you.

To answer, "Who are you?" is one of the greatest gifts of your journey and it starts with your brain.

Chapter One
Are you *Brain Brilliant*?

Being *Brain Brilliant* is about understanding how your own brain and mind operate. If you know more about the way your brain functions and fires and the manner in which your mind assimilates and accommodates your experiences you can gain huge benefits. Being *Brain Brilliant* is about understanding how others' brains and minds operate. If you know more about the way other people's brains are wired and working and the manner in which they might perceive and process the world around them you can gain huge benefits. By combining the knowledge of how your own mind operates with the insight of how others' minds might operate you can truly increase your personal and professional profit.

Are you ready for fundamental information about how to become more effective on the job and in your personal life? Are you ready for some cutting edge tips about how your brain really works and how the brains of other people really work? Are you ready for innovative applications most others still don't have? If so, this book is invaluable to you. The information in this book and the practical application of it in your personal and professional life will help you better understand your own perceptions, help you make better decisions, help you to better deal with conflict situations, help you attain your goals, help you develop your own leadership skills and help you take control of your own life.

So where do you begin? With your brain, of course. The following exercise introduces you to the basic manner in which your brain wires and fires.

Each arrow below represents a direction. Forward, right, left and backward respectively.

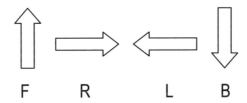

Say, out loud, the direction represented by each arrow in the row below. (If you are reading this book amongst a crowd, do it anyway, if you get a look, just say you're doing an exercise to grow your brain. It's true you are, though I promise it won't hurt.)

Ready…out loud!

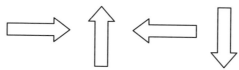

Terrific. Now stand up. Say, out loud, the direction represented by each arrow in the row below while simultaneously taking one small step in that same direction. For example, say right and step right at the exact same time and then move quickly to the next arrow. (Seated on an airplane? Shuffle your feet in the same direction, and keep your seatbelt fastened until the captain turns off the "Fasten Seat Belts" sign. Otherwise, you should be on your feet.)

Ready…out loud, and step or shuffle.

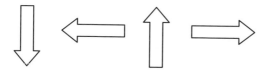

No congratulations as you should have learned this when you were three. However, now it starts to get challenging and interesting.

Stay standing (or keep shuffling) and say, out loud, the direction represented by each arrow in the next set while simultaneously taking one small step in the opposite direction. Then move quickly to the next arrow. For example, say left and step right at the exact same time.

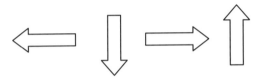

Bit flummoxed are you? Let's try it another way. Stay standing (or keep shuffling) and say, out loud, the opposite direction represented by each arrow in the row below while simultaneously taking one small step in the correct direction. Then move quickly to the next arrow. For instance, say backward and step forward at the exact same time.

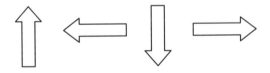

Not easy is it? If you wish to end positively return to what you know and are comfortable with by calling out the correct direction while simultaneously stepping or

shuffling in that same correct direction for the previous
set of arrows. Exercise completed.

**Why would I start a book on the fairly sophisticated
topic of your brain by having you participate in a
fairly unsophisticated exercise?** For the simple reason
that what your brain knows and practices becomes
habitual and automatic. For years you have practiced the
art of right and left. You literally move right, forward,
backward and left without bringing any conscious
thought to your actions. However, by doing the opposite
and involving physical movement your brain had to
adjust. Your brain optimized a "cross-lateral function"
(meaning the left and right movements of your body are
controlled by the opposite side of the brain) by
consciously rewiring in order to attempt the exercise.
You could not rely on the connections that normally fire
and wire because these connections no longer served the
purpose for completing this exercise successfully.

It's difficult to do something new. First you must figure
out the new information, then you add it or adjust it to
what you already know, and finally your brain rewires or
makes new connections all together in order to have this
new information become meaningful to you. When
you're outside of your comfort zone it can be confusing

and frustrating while you figure everything out. This is normal. We all like our ruts, routines and our grooves and so do our brains, but while your brain does like habits and routines, it actually prefers the new, the exciting and the out of the ordinary.

The second point of this exercise is that your brain has the capability of developing new connections, growing new cells and evolving up until the very day you breathe your last breath. Your brain grew in order to participate in this exercise. This exercise serves as the catalyst for realizing that your brain drives you and you can determine to a certain extent how to steer it. Unfortunately, you typically drive by habits, patterns, ruts and comfort zones.

So what does this exercise prove, other than how much you like the rut you're in? It proves you can move out of your ruts. You already have by attempting to teach your brain a new right and left pattern. Your brain is a constantly adapting, flexible machine that craves the new, the unusual, anything that requires it to create new neural connections.

Neural connections are the links between your brain's nerve cells. When nerve cells connect, your brain creates associations between ideas, thoughts and bits of information and these associations are what allow you to process and comprehend your surroundings. Every second of every day your brain is firing along its neural pathways in response to everything you perceive, process, think, feel and do. Every second of every day is an opportunity to consciously change some of these neural pathways that keep you from reaching your full potential or realizing your goals and dreams.

Your brain is comparable to being its own complex universe. It competes in a Darwinism of its own between all your neurons, killing off weaker unneeded cells and building upon those cells that you use regularly and that are needed for your own survival. Everything you do affects everything that follows so that your brain is continuously growing, adapting, changing and rewiring over and over again in order to stay alive and function at its best.

If your brain evolves due to experiences, how do genetics influence who you are? Genes, the biological ingredients that contribute to the recipe of You, contain the instructions for the foundation of your brain and therefore influence the initial development. To some extent, during formation, your genes tell your brain cells where to go and how to act, which other cells to talk to and where to migrate. However, the adaptability, flexibility and complex nature of an ever-changing brain prevents scientists from always being able to predict the exact response your brain may have to a specific genetic mutation. While we certainly know a great deal about many genetic influences on diseases and traits, it is vitally important to understand that the average brain equally evolves from perceived experiences.

Genetics are part of the picture, part of the recipe of You. Genetics define your brain's initial development and basic structures; essentially serving as the skeletal structure for your brain matter. However, the foods you eat, the people you surround yourself with, the physical activities you participate in, the books you read, the traumas and joys you experience, the aspirations and expectations you set for yourself, i.e. the life you lead, all serve to influence the more detailed operations and the day to day development of your brain: the day to day development of who you are.

What's the bottom line on becoming *Brain Brilliant*? Your brain is the driver of you. It is ultimately responsible for the way you perceive, reason, relate and express who you are to the rest of the world. It's time to maximize what you know about the only organ you have that can question itself. Learning and understanding more about how the brain fires and wires, how hormones influence the decisions you make, the conflicts you resolve or create and the stress you manage or endure can help you to view your personal and professional life with a whole new perspective. Why do you perceive and process information the way you do and how does this perception style impact your performance, your productivity and your motivation? Why do you purchase what you do, work better with one member of your team over another, enjoy the company of the neighbor three doors down but not the family living across the street?

Becoming *Brain Brilliant* is about becoming more aware of how you operate internally with yourself and how you operate externally with others. It's not just what you feel and think about the events you participate in but how you perceive the world around you and how you choose to take action based on your perceptions.

Ready to change a few neural pathways and get out of the ruts you're in? Good. Let's start with the basics of rut creation, your memory.

Chapter Two
What do you remember?

The emotional "stuff," the absurd "stuff," the intense "stuff" and the personally relevant "stuff." Think back to the last time you were driving your car. The radio was tuned to one of your favorite stations and a song started playing that transported you back in time. It was no longer present day but five years ago when you attended a relative's wedding, or three years ago when your nephew was born or last winter when your dear friend went through her divorce. The song pulls up certain events in your life because your memories are intertwined with the emotions that you experienced in relation to the significant event. If the song was played at the time of the event itself or was a popular tune when the event occurred it attaches itself to that specific incident.

When you hear a song from years prior, the music triggers the emotions you experienced, these emotions trigger your ability to recall the specific event, which then triggers your trip down memory lane.

How do popular songs trigger personal memories?
Your brain has two main types of cells, neuron and glial.
Nearly a hundred billion neurons (the cells that drive
your brain power) comprise approximately fifteen
percent of your brain. The other eighty-five percent of
your brain is comprised of glial cells, as well as other
cells with minor functioning roles. The glial cells are
most important because they support, feed and protect the
neurons. Each neuron may have anywhere from one to
ten thousand links, called synaptic connections, to other
neurons. A neuron is a messenger of data, serving as a
relay station to other neurons. Picture a tree trunk
(neuron) with a big branch (axon) with lots of sub-
branches (dendrites) and every time you put "two and
two together" one of these sub-branches (dendrites)
touches the tip of another branch (axon) to create an
axon-dendrite synaptic connection, and voila, your mind
is at work.

Hear an old song on the radio and thousands of dendrites
and axons that once touched and fused together to create
meaning when you first heard the song are re-connecting
and retrieving information as the neural pathways fire
once again. Your thoughts follow a sequential pattern of
retrieval as the dendrites wire and fire, though to most of
you it seems as if your mind is just wandering.

Your internal thoughts might sound like:
Hey, this was the song they played the summer before I went off to college, (more dendrites/axons connect), *which was the summer Sue fell in love with Mike and Sue decided she didn't want anything to do with me. What a moron I was for being so depressed over her. Amazing, I haven't heard this song in years,* (more dendrites/axons connect), *and Jack broke his arm in that fierce 3-on-3 basketball tournament,* (still more connections) *and Marty yelled at us for cheating. Was he ever hotheaded!*

On and on your thoughts continue as each new association triggers another piece of stored data. The particular thoughts recalled are retrieved because there is something unique about the information. Most information surrounding the tournament is forgotten. Typically you do not remember the generic day-to-day information that seemed all consuming at the time. The clothes, the meals, the phone calls verifying time and place and any other trivial data are filtered out by your brain as nonessential for long-term memory storage.

If the brain is a sponge, absorbing all sorts of information all the time, why can't you remember what you ate for lunch on the second Tuesday of last month? You can't remember because the brain is not a sponge. The sponge analogy is a myth. Your brain is really a sieve. The human brain can normally register over thirty-six thousand images per hour. Your eyes alone are designed to take in thirty million bits of information per second. The brain cannot possibly keep track of this large amount information, let alone store it for later retrieval.

Your brain retains approximately one percent of a day's activities and disregards the rest. It does this for survival. If you truly needed to know what you ate for lunch last Tuesday because of dietary or health issues you would remember, or at the very least, you would remember to write it down. However, for most of us it was literally a forgettable experience.

So what makes one percent stick? You remember information that is sensory associated, especially visual information. You remember experiences or information that is unusual, imaginative or exaggerated. Experiences that have intense emotions attached to them whether or not the emotions are positive or negative. Any information that is needed for survival in the future or is personally important and relevant to your ability to function is vital for storage in your long-term memory bank. Additionally, repetition plays a large role in remembering. Any type of information that is consistently repeated will typically remain for long-term retrieval.

What is even more amazing is that ninety-nine percent of the one percent you retain is learned non-consciously. This ninety-nine percent of the one percent means that the majority of what you learn is through your peripheral awareness and your perception filters. In other words, your brain, without conscious awareness, is constantly sensing, filtering, processing and choosing whether or not to store incoming data in your memory bank. Every new piece of data that you are introduced to through sight, sound, touch, taste, texture or intuition is processed, whether you consciously register the incoming data or not.

Example. Weeks after attending a large wedding, you normally cannot recall all the small details, unless you're a wedding planner in which all details are personally and professionally relevant and memorable to you. However, if not a wedding planner, you tend to remember that you visited with your cousin Jack whom you haven't seen in years, that you ate a little too much good food, that your back is still suffering from too many sudden moves on the dance floor and that you had a whopping great time.

What you've forgotten are the thousands of images and pieces of data your brain decided weren't worthy of keeping.

With over forty quadrillion (That's sixteen zeroes readers! 40,000,000,000,000,000) possible synaptic connections why can't you remember the name of the person you met just five minutes earlier? This phenomenon can be attributed to the common maxim "Use it or lose it." This phrase is true for much of what we remember and almost all of that which we forget. Dendrites connect with axons when meaning is created. Dendrites can stay connected with axons for several reasons, therefore making the connection needed and readily available to the brain. For example, in the introduction, "Hi, my name is Emily, it's nice to meet you," it would be far more helpful to the brain if we started or ended the phrase with the other person's name.

S: "Hi, I'm Susan."
E: "Hi, Susan, I'm Emily. It's really nice to meet you, Susan."

By repeating the name you reinforce the connection between the dendrite and the axon. Go one step further by saying the name a third time.

E: "So, Susan, is this your first time at this networking event?"

or

E: "I hear you're a teacher, Susan, which subject do you teach?"

You increase the likelihood that you'll remember the person's name the more you say it out loud. (Caution: three to four times is enough. If you say it too many times you may sound like a broken record.)

In addition to repetition, if you should discover that Susan graduated from the same college as one of your siblings, the percentage of retention considerably increases because now there is personal relevancy and additional connections in which to associate and connect Susan into pre-existing neural pathways.

If information is repeated often enough the dendrite and axon actually fuse together and create a permanent link. If infrequently or never used, the "branches" connect once or twice and forever more live separate lives. How many times have you run into someone you recognize and yet you cannot place his or her name? Instead of saying, "Hey, Susan, how are you?" you find yourself greeting the person with an over enthusiastic "Hi, how are You? How's life treating You?" It happens for several reasons. First, lack of repetition if it is a person you met once at a party and chatted with for only a few minutes. The more repetition, the more use. The stronger the connection between dendrite and axon, the more likelihood the connection will be fused. Second, the person's presence is out of context of where you originally met her or where you typically interact with her.

You remember information both as content and context. What the information is in itself (content) and where you learned or experienced it (context). For example, most of you work with a group of individuals, and you think you know the name of the woman who works nine desks over from you, until you see her at a ballgame, and darn it if you can't recall her name. Embarrassing, but normal operation for your brain.

In addition to repetition, what else makes connections fuse together so you remember and recall information? You are a sensory being absorbing the world around you through sight, sound, taste, touch, smell and intuition. You remember information that contains intense sensory associations. The taste of your favorite grandmother's recipe, the sight of your uncle's bright and outrageous shirts, the sight of your sister's smile, the sound of an older neighbor whistling, the touch of a dog's tongue licking your hand. The song on the radio mentioned earlier. Any sensory perception that is intense and possibly repeated is remembered.

Your brain also thrives on the new and distinctive for you are a naturally curious, eager learner. Anything that is outstanding or different stands out in your mind because it is unusual and unexpected. It takes your brain by surprise and thus it is more easily stored. Your mind is literally more engaged by the novel experience because new connections and associations are being created. For instance, the first time you go snow skiing your brain is reacting with a, "Whoa!" Your brain is accommodating a new and different experience. The twentieth time you go snow skiing at the same resort your brain reacts with a: "Ho-hum, this is the twentieth time I've seen this landscape and experienced this downhill slope."
While your brain may not be excited by the same experience, this repetition and familiarity with the task is exactly how skills develop. Incoming data that is unique stays upper most in your mind, literally residing in your neocortex until the newness fades. Once the information is automated it can be relegated to lower regions of the

brain where it is de-emphasized and filed away for years to come.

When you first learned how to drive it required complete focus and concentration. The skills required in this new experience resided in your neocortex. After practicing your driving skills on a regular basis you no longer needed to focus quite as much in order to get the same results. Suppose you are cruising along the interstate, listening to your favorite tunes and on your way to visit a friend who has just moved into a new neighborhood. You're doing fine following the written directions you've been given until you exit off the interstate and you start having to make a lot of neighborhood turns. Something doesn't seem quite right. What's the most typical reaction? Turning the volume of the radio down or off. Why? Because the driving skills that were automatic and allowed you to drive and listen to music at the same time have just now been replaced with higher order thinking skills such as problem solving and figuring out where you are in relation to your friend's house. These problem-solving skills require more focus and more neurons, thus causing you to reduce distractions such as music. Once you figure out you're headed in the right direction you turn the volume back up. With repeated trips to your friend's house you will automatically remember how to get there and the newness and novelty of the first trip wears off. The directions get relegated to a lower region of the brain, allowing you to leave the radio on until you reach the driveway.

Depending on how your brain fires and wires, you may memorize all the street names and easily recite directions to the house if needed by another, or you may forget half of the street names because you "automatically" know how to get there based on visual cues such as turning right at the oak tree, proceeding two blocks and then taking a left just after the gas station.

Either way, once the process becomes automatic your brain eagerly awaits for the next new destination.

How do you apply this retention information in a work environment? In a professional setting if you want someone to remember you or to remember your product, tell the person something unique or unusual (but appropriate) about you or your products and services. Explain what separates you from the thousands of others who are applying for the job or who are seeking to form a business relationship with the buyer's company. Explain what separates your product from the thousands of other items that essentially serve the same purpose.

Attach an emotional appeal for why the person should hire you and/or buy your product or services. Is it efficient and more effective therefore reducing this person's production time? Are your materials environmentally safer than any other company's products? Have you successfully worked with another prestigious company and therefore have a track record of excellence with very reputable businesses?

Appeal to at least three of the buyer's five senses. Include sight, sound, touch, smell and taste in your meeting to the extent that it makes sense and is appropriate. If selling soap, scent is a great appeal. If selling motor oil, skip the buyer's sense of smell and focus on other senses. Inform the buyer that the oil has the perfect viscosity for a high performance engine. Tell the buyer why and show the buyer how it works.

Repeat your key points and leave the buyer with a question to answer that incites the buyer to take positive action as well as reflect upon the benefit of having your product or service.

Example. Suppose you are selling a new software application. When introducing the product it is important to explain how the application complements the buyer's needs and seamlessly fits the type of work performed in her industry. Provide examples. Now you're making it personally relevant.

Next, what's the emotion attached to the purchase? Is it going to create better solutions and thus make her feel better for providing superior answers to her customers? Is it going to reduce time and make her more efficient in the eyes of her customers and/or make her feel better for being more productive? Is it going to cut costs and make her feel better about meeting her budget and increasing her profit margins? Is it going to build customer relations and hence make her feel good about building her business and growing her company's reputation? Is it going to reduce her stress and as a result make her feel better because it reduces her number of headaches? Identify the emotion, address it and leave the buyer feeling good about herself when working with you.

Appeal to the buyer's senses. Let her see the software application. (Visual) Let her manipulate various technical functions. (Touch) Let her listen to the solutions it provides as cited by you as well as any sounds directly emitted from the software itself. (Sound) Let her voice, in her own words, the benefits she thinks the application will provide for her.

Repeat your key points for serving her needs and highlight how your service or product outweighs the costs of not doing business with you. (Economists call this Opportunity Costs.)

Finally, ask her questions so that she may positively reflect on your product. How will this application increase her revenue? How might this application serve as a catalyst to building relationships with potential clients? How can her sales reps use this application out in the field to better drive sales? How would she feel if this product increased her third quarter sales by fifteen percent?

Questions trigger the brain to search for an answer. Our synapses wire and fire to create meaningful connections that can provide us with an acceptable answer to the question. Reflection and evaluation are the highest levels of cognitive thought, therefore reflective questions help you to create the most complex neural pathways in your brain as you search for an answer. These complex interconnected pathways help you retain information for the long haul.

Example: *What color is the box for the software application?* is a recall question, requiring the least amount of brain activity. You look at the box, you visually interpret green, and you say green. However, the question, *What would be the benefit to you and your sales consultants if you had a tool that could streamline your sales process for you?* asks for reflection and evaluation and causes a great deal of thought in the areas requiring analysis, comparison and prediction. By engaging a much larger number of neurons you boost the involvement process that in turn aids memory.

Questions are an amazing tool. (For more information on profit generating question ideas read Chapter Three.)

What else stands out for your memory bank? You tend to remember the first and last components within a session far more than you remember what happens in-between. Whether this session is 45 minutes or 90 minutes, you typically are more stimulated by what occurs first and last due to novelty (beginnings) and reflection and evaluation (endings).

With each new experience, according to psychologists, comes a new mental mind frame. The emotions, hormones and chemical changes that occur at the beginning of an experience are different than at the middle or end of an event, with the "middle" timeframe leading to continuity and possibly boredom. Beginnings provide new mental stimulation and endings provide reflection and evaluation (highest levels of thinking) or they may provide transitions to new beginnings thus creating a transition to new stimulation. Within this cyclical mentality, the average adult can stay focused on one type of experience or one type of incoming data for only twenty to twenty-five minutes.

How do twenty-minute cycles influence and increase your personal and professional profit? If you know your brain typically functions best in twenty-minute cycles there are many ways to improve your mental performance and raise your ability to be productive and focused.

Start managing your day by blocking longer chunks of time for various tasks into shorter timeframes. For instance, prioritize your tasks and responsibilities and then, as much as your job allows, try transitioning between these tasks so that your brain is stimulated in a variety of ways and therefore frequently gets re-energized by the switch in mental tasking.

Many of us can actually stay focused for hours when motivated and/or when a task requires a wide variety of skills needed in order to complete it. There can be a switching of mental states in the brain that occurs frequently enough that the brain stays stimulated and engaged for quite some time. However, if you typically engage in a single activity for more than twenty-five minutes your brain gets restless.

Give yourself "breaks" in-between tasks to re-stimulate and energize your brain. After typing at the computer for twenty to thirty minutes, get up and take a brief walk or deliver an item to someone rather than asking someone else to do it. Walk to the water fountain. Make needed phone calls. Vary what you do, but consciously create these breaks so that you still prioritize your responsibilities and maximize your time at hand.

In a learning situation, breaks give your brain time to accommodate (adjust) and assimilate (add) new information to what it already knows and understands. By taking a break from an intense learning situation or an intense work session you allow your mind to relax. You provide time for your brain to sift through the information and process the information more effectively. Ever step away from a crossword puzzle only to return to it sometime later and come up with a solution almost instantaneously, whereas before you were almost ready to tear your hair out in frustration? Classic results of brain "break."

If you frequently conduct meetings start providing more beginnings and endings. Transition between topics every twenty to twenty-five minutes. (For more ideas on conducting meetings read Chapter Three.)

When interviewing set up the meeting in twenty minute phases. For example, when interviewing a potential candidate for a sales position, divide the interview into three to five twenty-minute sessions. One session for a presentation given by the interviewee, one session for questions, one session for evaluation of the presentation and another session or two for incorporating the components that are needed to properly assess them for the position in which you are seeking a candidate.

Using the prior software application example, you could add additional components to the process of transitioning your potential customer into a client by knowing that your potential client will remember the first part of the meeting and the last part of the meeting far more than she will remember anything in-between. What do you say first? Do you start off with boring features and benefits or with engaging questions that stimulate her to start participating in the meeting? Do you close your time with the potential customer with positive impressions and questions for her to reflect upon? Do you get her to take action? Do you help her think about what she might say when she goes back to discuss your product or service with her colleagues? Or do you say, "Thank you, have a great day" and miss an opportunity to have her remember you?

What's the bottom line on remembering?
You remember best:

- Through Sensory Associations, Especially Visual
- By Emotions Attaching to Significant Events or Data
- By Experiencing Outstanding, Unique, or Different Qualities in a Situation or at an Event
- Through Information That is Needed for Your Personal or Professional Survival
- Through Information That is Personally Relevant and Immediately Applicable in Your Life
- Through Repetition
- By Taking Breaks
- Through Information and Experiences That Are First and Last in a Session
- Did I Mention Repetition?!

Chapter Three
Why ask questions?

The brain triggers on questions not statements.

If you are one of the lucky few that actually manages to still be diligently working on your New Year's resolutions in February, I'm impressed. If you are like the millions of people who, by January 19th, cannot even remember what your New Year's resolutions were, let alone what you're suppose to be doing to achieve them, it's because your brain was never optimally triggered.

Resolutions in themselves are set up for failure just by calling them *resolutions*. What's the definition of a resolution? Technically, according to the dictionary, it's the state of being resolute or determined. However, from a brain perspective it's being stubborn enough to "re-solution" the same goal year after year. In other words, the first attempt at finding a solution didn't work, so hey, why not repeat the same exact statement and expect different results this year. Yikes!

Your subconscious mind responds to questions far better than it responds to statements or wishes. If you turn a statement, resolution or goal into a question you can trigger your brain to take action because the first thing it will naturally want to do is answer the question.

How do questions trigger action and increase your personal and professional profit? While you are a naturally curious human being and therefore love to learn, you are never quite as thrilled with being told what to do or being told the significance of an historical event, as much as you like being asked to do something or as much as you like being asked what impact you think the historical event has had on your life today.

When you ask yourself questions or are asked questions by others, the question itself will trigger your brain's synapses and these synapses will wire and fire to create meaningful connections that provide you with an answer to the question.

If you have ever set a goal, personally or professionally, you know how difficult it can be to reach it. By setting goals through the formation of questions you can incite your brain to take action toward reaching the goal and increase the likelihood that you will attain it.

Read the following statements:
I want to lose 15 pounds.
I want to read more books.
I want to increase my sales by 8% this quarter.
I want to improve customer retention.
I want a more positive relationship with my teenager.
I want to find a better job.
I want to be happier.
I want to attain a more stable financial picture for myself.

All of these statements are understandable and admirable goals, but none of them incite action. By re-wording them into questions they will trigger your brain into generating more questions. These questions will generate still more questions, and these multiple questions will lead to more finite action steps as you move toward the solution.

Sample statements re-worded as questions:
I want to lose 15 pounds.
Vs.
How am I going to lose 15 pounds?
What do I need to do in terms of a diet plan? What resources can help me create a nutritional plan that works for my lifestyle? Who can I go see? What books are available to help? What can I do to exercise more? Who has had great success in this area? What worked for

them and could it work for me? What reward/payoff do I get from my current eating habits? How can I replace my current behaviors with different behaviors that help me get the results I seek and still offer me a "reward" but in a healthier way? What steps have I taken before that actually worked? How can I build upon these successes? How will losing weight improve my health? What will be the benefit to my family? What will be the benefit to me?

How might I increase my sales by 8% this quarter? What resources do I need? What am I already doing that works well? How can I build upon these strengths? Who has excellent sales strategies? What makes their strategies so successful? What resources can I read about to help me achieve this percentage increase? Who is my best client currently? What about this relationship makes it so positive? What have I already done to retain this client for as long as I have? What will be the benefits to me if I increase my sales? What will be the benefits to my team, to the company?

Whatever goal you seek, re-word it as a question and then ask yourself the following:

- What skills, information and knowledge do I need to achieve this goal?

- What resources, assistance, and/or collaboration do I need to achieve this goal?
- What assumptions and obstacles can block the progress of achieving this goal?
- What "underlying need" of the "surface want" will be met when I achieve this goal? (Read Underlying Needs chart in Chapter 4.)
- What do I already do that works well? How can I build upon these successes and strengths?
- When I actually achieve this goal, what will be the benefit to me? To others?

Using these follow-up questions to support the initial question will allow your brain to make more and more connections, creating a greater number of links between a wider range of thoughts and possible solutions. Questions stimulate cognitive thought and increase your solution seeking capabilities.

Now that you have a questioning technique for reaching your goals it is quite likely that you will increase the probability of attaining them, with one caveat: you have to actually apply the tool by asking and answering the questions.

When else can you apply questions to increase your professional profit? When can you not?! Team meetings, problem-solving situations, resolving conflict, decision making, creativity, performance and production, interviews, evaluations and just about every component of the working world can benefit from the use of questions.

Most meetings are a waste of everyone's time. Especially when they focus on who left the dishes in the community sink, who jammed the copy machine, what went wrong on the deal, why the proposal was rushed and who can take all the blame. Ugh. You might as well have walked over to the toilet and watched a few thousand dollars swirl around the bowl before disappearing out of sight. At least that would have been slightly entertaining.

Meetings are prime opportunities to generate higher levels of performance and productivity, to share visions, to generate new ideas, to help individuals and groups find internal motivation, to have people feel accepted and valued, to identify strengths and successes, to build upon these successes and to incite action.

What if the agenda items for your next meeting were questions? What if these questions incited higher level thinking skills and sparked new ideas, approaches, methodologies and systems? What would be the benefit if these questions increased individual participation and stimulated people into action? What would be the benefit of a meeting where people left feeling valued, motivated and intellectually challenged? What would be the benefit of a meeting where individuals left with specific action plans generated by themselves in order to meet a collective vision?

The next time you hold a meeting, create an agenda of questions. If it's a business development meeting try building upon past successes by asking team members about past successes. What made these successes so great? You can even have your team help you incorporate questions into the proposals themselves to help trigger the minds of the potential client.

When conducting a sales meeting, ask your team what their individual and collective strengths are and how they can share what's working for them with others? Ask them what their goals are, and then have them rewrite them in the form of questions. Ask them what the benefits will be when they reach their goals. Ask them who they are targeting and why and what plan of approach they have created.

How can questions be used to generate new ideas or creative solutions? When conducting a brainstorming session have every answer be in the form of a question. This is incredibly beneficial for generating innovative ideas and discovering new approaches. Break people into small groups or pairings and hand each group a question. Allow eleven to seventeen minutes for everyone to generate ten to fifteen more questions as their answer to the original question.

Example: One group gets assigned, *What is the definition of leadership?* Another group receives, *What is an Ideal Client Relationship?* and another group starts with, *What is communication?* and on and on. Assign one question per group for as many groups as you have participating. Each group then brainstorms ten to fifteen more questions in order to help them come up with a better answer to the assigned question.

When assigned, *What is communication?* the group might generate such questions as:
- Where can/does communication break down?
- Why might some people be better communicators than others?
- Which methods of communication might be more effective in certain circumstances?

- How do different types of relationships effect communication?
- What are the components/ingredients of good conversations?
- Which modes of communication do people perform best? Like best?
- How do good communicators convey their messages clearly?

In the process of answering a question with more questions you elicit extended ideas, thoughts and connections. Questions provide a context for developing a more creative, more detailed answer. Question brainstorming may broaden perspective and lead to an answer that would never have been generated if the typical question and statement -answer format had been used.

Are all questions good questions? No. Unfortunately, all of us have heard negative questions such as, *What's the problem here?, Why on Earth did you do that?, Whose fault was it?, Why are we so inefficient with this process?* Questions that are negative, condescending and seek blame are not helpful. Questions that seek to focus on yesterday's failures and not today's and tomorrow's successes only perpetuate failure. Questions that move forward positively, questions that help individuals and teams identify strengths and foundations upon which to build, questions that generate new ideas and improved approaches are questions that lead to personal and professional profit. Profit for the individual, for the team, for the organization and for everyone involved.

What's the bottom line question on using questions? Using the question method not only eliminates that "resolution" mentality, it also creates a course of action that enhances your opportunity for success.

What would be the benefit to your team, to your company, to your friends, to your family and to you if you used profit-generating questions in your life?

Chapter Four
What are your underlying needs?

Underlying needs are the drivers of goal setting, resolution statements, aspirations and questions. They are internal motivation factors that directly contribute to your behaviors.

If you go back and re-read the previous chapter's goal statements, you will notice that all of them are written with the word *want*. This wording is representative of the way the majority of people set goals. You set them based on what you think you want, but you do so without confirming what it is you truly need.

Writing your goals in the form of questions is only half of the equation. Reaching your goal may still leave you feeling unfulfilled if you focus on the "surface want" of your goal and not the "underlying need" of your goal. The "surface want" is what your brain consciously verbalizes and the "underlying need" is your brain's subconscious foundation for why you really want what you do.

For instance, "surface wants" might include that you want to increase your sales this quarter, you may want Mary to like you, or that you may want to go on a vacation. The "underlying needs" may actually be that you need to feel successful, that you need to prove to yourself or others that you know what you're doing, that you need to feel accepted or valued by another person, or that you are stressed to the gills and need a mental and physical change of scenery. The underlying need explains why it is that you want what you do.

Therefore, it is essential that you clarify the result you truly seek and what underlying need you are meeting by reaching this goal. If you do take the time to identify the correct underlying need, not only will you be satisfied when you attain the goal, but in the process of working toward your goal you will have higher levels of internal motivation.

How do underlying needs work in the sales process? Every sales professional (including you - as explained below) needs to know the sixteen cross sections between Life Sectors and the Four Levels of Need. Knowing these cross sections allows the sales person to identify all of the possible needs of the potential buyer. If the sales professional meets the surface wants of the customer, but fails to meet the underlying needs of the customer, the sales professional will not retain the customer. In fact, the customer may be so disillusioned with attaining the "surface want" and not attaining the "underlying need," that not only does the customer cut off all ties with the sales professional, but the customer also starts talking poorly about the sales professional and his company. Even though the customer supposedly got what he was seeking to buy (and perhaps even at a ten percent discount) he still may feel dissatisfied.

Why do you still need to know about Underlying Needs in the sales process if you don't sell professionally? Even if you are not in sales for a career, you are a sales person every day of your life. You are constantly selling your ideas, solutions and even your attitude to others. Perhaps rather than convincing someone to buy widgets, you need them to pass legislation in your county or state or you need them to accept your suggestions at a neighborhood, school or church meeting. No matter what you may be selling in your daily life, it is necessary to target needs.

Even more important than selling personal or professional ideas to others, you are constantly selling ideas to yourself. You are continuously in the position of convincing yourself that the choices that you are making are the right ones, that they are in your best interest for healthy physical, emotional, intellectual and spiritual growth. To sell to yourself properly (and appropriately) you need to know your own underlying needs. The matrix below explains how the four main sectors of your life, including family and friends, a partner, your professional arena and your own individual growth overlap four levels of essential needs.

Life Sectors

		Family/Friends	Partner	Professional	Self
4 Levels of Need	Physical	Family/Friends Physical	Partner Physical	Professional Physical	Self Physical
	Emotional	Family/Friends Emotional	Partner Emotional	Professional Emotional	Self Emotional
	Intellectual	Family/Friends Intellectual	Partner Intellectual	Professional Intellectual	Self Intellectual
	Spiritual	Family/Friends Spiritual	Partner Spiritual	Professional Spiritual	Self Spiritual

What are your underlying Physical needs? Your Physical needs include maintaining an optimal level of health by caring for and respecting your physical body. An ideal physical condition is different for different people based on physical limitations, body type and/or personal needs. By providing for your individual dietary and medical needs and by managing proper sleep and stress levels (For more information on managing stress read Chapter Seven) you can create physical wellness for yourself.

Physical needs also include your environmental needs at home and at work. How much space you have to spread out your "stuff" at work and still feel at the top of your game, to the color of the walls, to furniture placement, to decorating style, to temperature all determine the extent to which your needs are being met. The make-up of the spaces you frequently occupy determines the level to which your Physical needs are met in your surroundings.

Physical needs also include the geographic distances and the levels of proximity you need with others. How close you need to live to your relatives in order to feel secure but independent, the distance between your home and the homes of friends, bosses, and/or colleagues are all part of Physical needs.

Finally, Physical needs also include the level of intimacy you receive from relationships. These relationships range in closeness from strangers, to acquaintances, to colleagues, to friends, to family and to a partner. What is an acceptable level of proximity with others at some of these levels is often culturally influenced, but each of you has your own imaginary bubble around you and you frequently get irritated when someone bursts it without asking. From handshakes to pats on the back, to hugs to your own sexuality, Physical needs for intimacy are highly individualized. Know where your boundaries are and communicate them clearly. Listen to others when they tell you about their boundaries and respect them. Know what you need from a partner and communicate clearly. Listen to your partner when s/he tells you about his/her needs and respect these needs. Compromise if necessary; seek outside support if necessary, but it is key to start with questions. It is incredibly difficult to create a win-win scenario in a relationship if you don't even know what you need.

For instance, in a partner relationship, ask yourself: *What do I need? What does my partner need, (as indicated by your partner)? What is considered acceptable and appropriate to us both? How can we get both individual's needs met if they are slightly different? Where can*

58

compromise and negotiation come into play without either partner losing a fundamental need? What's the benefit to each of us if we find an acceptable way to meet both of our needs?

What are your underlying Emotional needs? Your underlying Emotional needs are generated when you create relationships with others and with yourself. When you enter into a relationship (personal, professional, fleeting, short-term or long-term) with another person, that individual will directly contribute to your emotional state, either positively or negatively or both.

As strange as it may sound, you also have a relationship with your Self that determines your emotional needs in the area of self-esteem or self-value and these needs influence your self-concept.

The "Acceptance" of your Emotional needs directly influences your self-esteem and your self-concept. Self-esteem is how you view yourself and the unique set of skills and talents you possess. Self-concept is the value placed on your view. You might be a fantastic tennis player. Your incredible skill causes you to have high self-esteem. However, if your parents or peers do not value your athletic ability and/or you do not value it, your

59

self-esteem in this one area might be high, but your overall self-concept might be low.

Your ability to effectively manage your own emotions, to effectively manage the emotions of others, your ability to accept the wide range of emotions you experience throughout your life and your ability to productively and positively manage your emotional relationships with others and the emotional relationship you have with yourself all determine how well your Emotional needs are met.

What are your underlying Intellectual needs? Your underlying Intellectual needs include a need for self-awareness in regard to your own core beliefs and an understanding and respect of these beliefs by others. Intellectual needs also include your cravings for challenging and stimulating mental growth opportunities, and respect for this acquired knowledge in yourself by you and others. Finally, you need individual clarity on your own cerebral strengths, weaknesses, areas of expertise and areas of being a novice.

You are a life long learner. You crave stimulation and new opportunities to learn. Constantly. An ideal intellectual life is different for different people based on interests, curiosities, opportunities and personal needs, but we all seek and need to learn new knowledge throughout our lives. By feeding your cravings for new learning opportunities you can create an environment that stimulates your brain.

What are your underlying Spiritual needs? Your underlying Spiritual needs include creating a value system for your actions and choices. This is a foundational component for every level of need, but most especially with Spiritual needs, so I place it here. Only when there is an alignment of values and actions can you begin to meet your needs for ethics, integrity and morality. Finding acceptance of your value system is also a Spiritual need.

Meeting Spiritual needs includes finding strength in a Higher Source, no matter what term you may use to identify and refer to the Source. The Higher Source you believe in provides you strength. It is a resource to help you serve yourself so that you may better serve others.

What is the purpose of identifying underlying needs? By asking questions, digging deeper, finding the root and clarifying the issues you will understand why you want certain things, what the real benefits will be when you attain your goals and you will know how real satisfaction and fulfillment feel.

How do you even begin to know what your underlying needs are, let alone what the underlying needs are of others? Ask questions. When figuring out your own needs, use the Clear Cognitive Connection chart below. It is a great tool. The process of creating a Clear Cognitive Connection is the process of getting a "clear" picture of your wants and underlying needs which are your "cognitive" thoughts, and then "connecting" this "clear" picture to your daily choices and actions.

What is the overriding question for a Clear Cognitive Connection? What do I need on each of the four levels and in each of the four sectors, and how many of my needs are already being met?

In other words, what do you need Physically, Emotionally, Intellectually and Spiritually? What do you need from family and friends, from a partner, from your job and from yourself in each of these four sectors? Are you getting what you need some of the time, all the time, or hardly ever? This overriding question forces you to take inventory of your current reality. If you know what you need and the level to which your needs are currently being met you can create a better action plan for moving forward and increasing your personal and professional profit.

How does creating a Clear Cognitive Connection increase your personal and professional profit? Creating a Clear Cognitive Connection allows you to develop a concise, unique action plan for moving forward positively and productively.

After you take inventory by answering the overriding question, you may be stoked that you're doing really well in meeting the majority of your needs, or you may be slightly bummed by the fact that you're getting very few of your needs met. This is absolutely okay, and exactly why you're taking an inventory in the first place. You need to simply 'Accept' that this is where you're at today. This is also a prime opportunity to quit beating yourself up and start looking at your mistakes as lessons you have learned. Viewing life as a series of exciting challenges and learning opportunities rather than as a series of obstacles and mistakes helps you move forward more positively by helping your brain let go of all the old baggage and old neural connections in order to focus on creating new possibilities and new neural connections.

Clear Cognitive Connection Chart

What do I need on each of the four levels and in each of the four sectors, and how many of my needs are already being met?

Awareness of 4 Levels	Where am I at currently, in meeting each of my needs within each of the 4 Levels, and within each Sector of my life?
Acceptance of 4 Levels	It's okay to be exactly where I'm at in meeting my needs, b/c the experiences that I have had thus far have brought me to where I am today. **Accepting me as I am today, what positive lessons have I already experienced that can help me step forward?**
Self Immunity	Determining your own needs and not having your needs dictated by others gives you self-immunity. Immunity is granting yourself the freedom to be who you are and to express your individuality. **Are my needs the needs of others, or do my needs represent and reflect me?**
Developing an Internal Balance	Accepting polarities and honoring pairs. We are capable of feeling and needing many supposedly opposing traits. You can be both powerful and vulnerable, have a desire to give as well as receive, and be both youthful and wise. **Do my needs reflect balanced traits?**
Effecting from Tranquility	Your actions and behaviors in the external world are determined by the inner peace you have with each of the sixteen areas of underlying needs. **Do my actions and behaviors reflect a true understanding of my needs?**

Once you have asked yourself the overriding question for a Clear Cognitive Connection and you know your needs, take a closer look at them. How many of these needs are your own, and not the needs of your parents, teachers, colleagues, boss or others who may influence you? Sometimes it's difficult to separate our needs from the needs of others, but you need to make sure that what you want and need is truly determined by you. If you're studying to be a doctor is it because you want to be a doctor and you're fulfilling your need to serve others or is it because your mother never finished medical school and needs you to complete her unfulfilled desires? While it may seem slightly melodramatic, you may be going after wants and needs that have been more influenced by the needs of others than the needs of your own mind. Case in point, have you ever been pressured to take part in something that you didn't really want to take part in? Enough said.

Next, you need to assess the level to which your identified needs help you lead a healthy life. Do your underlying needs represent a balance of traits? Do you allow yourself to play and work, or is your life driven by the need for professional accomplishments and praise? Do you give as well as receive, or do you feel guilt the moment someone tries to help you for a change? While you cannot ever find balance with life's daily activities (Read Chapter Seven) you can create an internal balance of needs. This is incredibly important to your own mental and physical well-being.

Lastly, do your actions and choices reflect your needs? Do you make choices to consciously seek out more of what you need? Do you react to certain circumstances or another human being in a certain way and do you understand why you react the way you do? What do your reactions and thoughts reflect back to you about your own unmet needs?

What's the bottom line on figuring out your Underlying Needs and creating a Clear Cognitive Connection? Your underlying needs, not your surface wants, drive you and the choices you make. Every time you create a goal (in the form of a question) also ask yourself what need it is that you're really trying to fulfill. Knowing your needs and why you behave the way you do automatically increases your understanding and awareness of you. That's profit!

Chapter Five
What is a rational decision?

An oxymoron. You make decisions every day from what shirt to wear, what to eat for lunch, who to praise, who to criticize, where to go on vacation, who to sign the deal with and what brands you will buy. You typically assume that your decisions have been based on your rational ability to weigh the pros and cons, to do the research, to check the facts and to obtain and compare the most current data. At the conclusion of all your efforts, you then make an auspicious announcement: "I am vacationing in the Caribbean this year," or "I am choosing a four-door sedan."

Making this so-called *rational* decision is a contradiction with how your brain works. It may very well be true that all of your data concludes that the Caribbean is the best financial choice for your next vacation, but there's no way you're packing your bags and heading for those crystal blue-green waters if you really desire to be munching on tacos in Texas. There's no way you're going to purchase the four-door sedan unless you feel good about how it's going to meet the needs of your lifestyle and how safe you're going to feel in it.

Furthermore, you're certainly going to hesitate about signing any deal with a company that proves on paper it can handle the work if you do not feel comfortable with the people you'll be collaborating with throughout the project, and you're certainly going to hesitate before you take on one more volunteer activity in the neighborhood if all you receive as feedback is whining complaints.

Through MRI studies (Magnetic Resonance Imaging -a technique that can take pictures of your brain or other parts of your body) and PET scans (positron emission tomography – an imaging procedure that looks at metabolic activity rather than anatomical structure) we now know that the *rational*, logical, decision making areas of your neocortex get a little help from other parts of the brain before making a final verdict.

Why is *rational* not the best modifier for describing the decisions you make? The brain is highly complex, and large volumes have been written on its intricacies, but for the purpose of a concise, clear and simplified understanding, it can be described in three main sections, commonly referred to by doctors and educators as the Triune brain.

Each section of the Triune brain has its own neuro-structure and its own set of responsibilities. The Stem or Reptilian region is located at the base of the brain. The stem/reptilian region is responsible for your safety and survival, and the well known "fight or flight" response we have in dangerous situations. If someone were to throw a brick at your head, the stem/reptilian region of your brain does not wonder how much the brick weighs, or how fast it might be traveling, or what the impact might be if the brick were to connect with your forehead. The reptilian region is wired for instinctive survival and very quickly and simply tells your body to duck!

The mid-section of your brain is referred to as the Limbic/Mammalian region. It performs four major tasks, one of which is the regulation of your biorhythms, which includes such functions as body temperature, blood pressure and heart rate. The second task it controls is your immune system, keeping you healthy. Memory and emotions are the last of the four tasks this section controls. You could not survive without the limbic/mammalian region, as it is the hub for how you respond to the world.

The fact that the same region of the brain that controls your emotions also controls your immune system explains why much of your emotional reactions show up in physical manifestations throughout your body. If someone compliments you on your beauty you blush. If you have a significantly stressful day within seventy-two hours you typically experience the common cold, a headache, a sore throat, a pain in your lower back or some other physical symptom that indicates to you that you are experiencing high levels of stress. If you start to experience feelings of nervousness your stomach flutters or your bowels tighten or your hands begin to sweat. With the same region of the brain controlling your emotions and your bodily functions relating to sleep patterns, your levels of hunger and your overall physical health, it is vitally important to know how to manage one's own feelings in order to maintain optimal levels of mental and physical performance.

The third and top area of the Triune brain is referred to as the Neocortex or the higher-level-thinking region of the brain. It is the spaghetti looking section that we see in drawings and pictures. It has many responsibilities as well, including but not limited to: language, cognitive skills, reasoning and behavior. The neocortex represents approximately eighty percent of the volume of your overall brain. This region is the part of the brain that analyzes, contemplates, digests information and solves problems. Along with the other two regions of the Triune brain, the neocortex processes millions of bits of data every hour, sorting and organizing it and deciding whether or not to send it to long-term memory storage.

The neocortex is responsible for making decisions, and since this region of the brain houses your ability to analyze and rationalize you might tend to think you can therefore make *rational* decisions. The fallacy of this assumption comes into play when you watch the brain fire and wire and you realize the neocortex is highly dependent upon the mammalian/limbic region.

The mammalian region houses feelings along with your memories, and it passes the emotion-laden information up to the neocortex where the information gets added to the other data being used in the present moment to make a decision. The neocortex accepts the information given to it by the mammalian/limbic region and adds it the pool of information it is using to determine some sort of solution. Therefore, every *rational* decision, supposedly based on hard cold data and logic, is actually influenced by emotions and feelings. Influenced by the same emotions and feelings that were generated from prior experiences (memories) that are associated with the current situation.

How does understanding that there is no such thing as a *rational* decision increase your personal and professional profit? Professionally, you can't sell your product or services nor will you buy someone else's product or services on the sole basis of features and benefits. There is an emotional basis in the purchasing and selling process. (Read Chapter Six for more information on the foundations of selling.)

Moreover, when you establish a new vision or mission statement for your company or team, when you create a new system or organizational process or when you write a job description or perform any professional task, take time to determine what emotions may be involved throughout the completion of a task, what emotions might hinder the process or what emotions might be associated with the current situation based on your probable past experiences or the prior experiences of your colleagues. By realizing that emotions play a key role in decision-making you can proactively address them in order to create more positive outcomes.

Likewise, the personal decisions you make all have an emotional foundation, and if you are not sure which emotions are coming into play in a given circumstance you will perform a disservice to yourself. The emotions and feelings you associate with specific situations, products, services or even people directly influence your ability to make the best decision for yourself.

Example. Suppose you had a job offer that required you to move your place of residence. Your decision to take the job or not isn't going to be solely based on the features and benefits of the new job. The mammalian part of your brain will add an emotional element based on your prior experiences and feelings with new jobs, with job transitions, with the process of moving itself, with the new geographic area you would be moving to, with the effect it would have on your family and friends and with the changes in lifestyle the entire process would create. Even if you believe your sole focus to be on an incredible raise in salary, therefore you're moving as fast as you can, it's actually the emotional view you have about the salary increase, not the logical view, that propels you to take action.

The decisions you make may will continually leave you unfulfilled or dissatisfied if you race through the decision making process completely focused on the *rational* side of the data. With the realization that you purchase products and services with emotions and that you sell your own products, services, ideas, strategies and perspective to others based on your emotions and their emotions gives you tremendous strength in attaining more of what you really need and want.

Example. Have you ever made a decision using logical reasoning only to regret your choice of action or your thoughts shortly thereafter? What seemed logical at the time just didn't seem intuitively right later.

Have you ever bought an item on impulse only to regret the purchase a few days later? In the moment, you think you need the item, only when you get it you still feel less than satisfied. This dissatisfaction in your decisions comes from the fact that either your underlying emotional need behind the decision did not get met, or your emotional state at the time you made the decision influenced your actions and you weren't consciously aware of the influence. In other words, the rational decision you thought you were making can be positively or negatively influenced by your prior experiences and the emotions you have about these experiences, your emotional state at the time of making the decision, by your emotional perspective about the people or ideas involved, or by your own emotional needs at the time.

The next time you make a major decision ask yourself:

Do I have any prior experiences that will influence my perspective about this current situation?

Do I have a positive or negative viewpoint toward anyone or anything involved in this situation that influences my decision?

Do I have a personal emotional need that I'm trying to meet at the time I make this *rational* decision? Am I making this decision because I need to feel better or I need to feel more in control?

Consider the previous car example mentioned at the beginning of this chapter. The fact that you are purchasing a four-door sedan is influenced by your emotions. While you do indeed consider the various features and benefits of many different brands, your mind is also considering safety, style, color and the prior brands you have driven and whether or not you enjoyed them. If your budget is tight, perhaps you can't have the first car on your list, but rather than giving up completely you'll start to emotionally compromise with yourself until you find a car that you can still feel good about purchasing.

Example #2. Have you ever asked for an increase in budget or income or been asked to increase another's budget or salary? If you're the person doing the requesting, typically you ask for this increase in money and you cite all the reasons your department needs it. You produce charts and graphs and explain how the money will be used. What you frequently leave out is the appeal to the emotions that are involved by the person making the decision to grant you more money.

Flip it around. If you are the person frequently receiving these requests, you have to endure all the charts and graphs and supposedly make a *rational* decision as to whether or not you think it's a good idea to start handing over more funds. What you need emotionally to make the decision is usually missing.

How can this become a win-win situation no matter whether you're asking for money or granting it? Incorporate emotions. If you have a proven track record for handling money responsibly, if you've shown where your current funds have been used and how this utilization has created an enviable return-on-investment then bring up the ideas of being responsible and trustworthy. Help the person granting you the money to feel confident in your abilities, to feel that she can trust you to create a successful outcome, and to know that you are humble enough that should you need help in the future you'll ask and not wait until all funds have been misappropriated.

If granting money, ask questions that help you attain information on the reliability, responsibility and maturity of the person to whom you plan on handing a check. Do they have prior experience, or do they have an eagerness, passion and financial skill level to support a first time increase? Where are their levels of integrity? Do their colleagues respect them? Do team members view this person as a trusted leader? Do you trust them?

What's the bottom line on decision-making? By understanding how your emotions influence your thought processes you increase your ability to make better decisions for yourself and you increase your ability to positively influence the decision making process of others. (Known as the art of persuasion and not to be misconstrued as manipulation.)

Whether your feelings or the feelings of others are positive or negative, having a greater awareness of them will help you better identify the emotional needs that underscore the decisions you and they make. When you

77

make better decisions you increase your own confidence and self esteem levels. That's a great profit.

Chapter Six
What are you really selling?

The same two things over and over again.

Regardless of whether you're in sales professionally or not, you sell every day of your life. If you're going to a job interview, requesting a raise, pitching an idea, asking someone to lend a hand, negotiating terms or persuading someone to take any action that helps you, you are selling.

At some point in time during a typical day you have tried to sell someone something. From products and services to ideas or concepts, the systems, schemes and pleas you continuously put forth to persuade someone else to act has consumed tremendous time and energy. Consider the latest professional sales seminars covering such topics as Territory Management, Responding to Buyer Reactions and Phone Call Cycles, and the latest personal "sales" seminars covering such topics as "Finding Your Mate in Aisle Eight," or "Being Perfect in Two Hundred Twenty-Six Easy Steps." Selling yourself or some thing reaches into all aspects of life.

With hundreds of books on the shelves espousing "How to Close the Deal," "How to Sell Your Child on the Idea of a Clean Room" "How to Act as a Consultant and Win the Client," "The Top 10 Tips of Successful Sellers," yaddy, yaddy, yaddy, there are few of you who haven't tried some new fan-dangled selling strategy in some way shape or form. It's easy to see or not see the results of trying the latest and greatest technique. The sale is closed or not. But have you ever wondered what selling is really about? What goes on underneath the surface of the seller-buyer relationship? Why one sale ends satisfactorily and another does not?

To answer these questions requires a very different perspective on the entire nature of selling. The majority of existing sales support information shares a similar detrimental perspective by essentially ignoring the single most important factor of the entire selling process: the brain. These seminars and books peddle theories for improving your sales without granting any consideration to the minds involved. Unfortunately, these pie chart, flow-chart approaches to selling are stifling if you are seeking to make serious strides in reaching and exceeding your sales goals. To make true changes in your sales requires understanding and knowledge of the machine that determines your customer's perceptions and behaviors in the first place. It requires taking on a whole new selling perspective: a neuro-sales perspective.

Why do people buy? Whether you're selling widgets or waffles or whiffle balls, people purchase your product or service for only two reasons. First, it provides a solution to their problem. A solution that meets the underlying need and not the surface want.

For example, take the person who walks into a store in order to purchase a sweater. The want is the sweater, but what is the underlying need? Is the sweater going to help keep him warm, help him look and feel more handsome thus increasing his self-esteem and confidence or is it being purchased to prove to his mother that he does in fact know how to dress himself? Remember the old cliché about the person who walks into a hardware store wanting to buy a drill? The person wants a drill but really needs what? A hole, and she needs the hole because she's trying to put something together or fix something or build something. The person who wants to buy any product or service has an underlying need that the product or service can fulfill. What would be the underlying need of the person who wants to purchase insurance? Security? Insurance for assurance? If people want your product or service, what is the underlying need they seek? If they don't even know they want your product, how do you get them to want it? By helping them identify a need they were not aware they had.

Second, people decide to buy your product or service because it creates good feelings. Most importantly, it creates good feelings about themselves. It makes them feel happy, proud, confident, hopeful or perhaps even ecstatic, but the bottom line is that a positive feeling is generated about themselves.

How do emotions get involved with deciding to buy? The neocortex is the part of the brain that houses your higher level thinking skills such as analysis, debate, evaluation, reasoning and decision-making. As stated in the previous chapter, before the cells in your neocortex wire and fire, they wire and fire through a section of the brain known as the mammalian/limbic region. The mammalian part of your brain serves as the control center of your emotions and memory. Every time you or your potential customer makes a "logical, analytical" decision to buy, the brain wires and fires through the mammalian section first so that an emotion can be carried to the neocortex. Before this section of the brain finally decides what action to take in any given circumstance it adds to the equation the information provided by the mammalian region.

If you want the potential customer to buy a product or service from you, you typically begin listing the benefits of your product over another and the top five reasons every person should purchase your widget. However, if the customer's going to make the "logical" decision to purchase widgets from you, the customer has to have a positive emotion associated with the purchase. In order for the customer to finally say, "Yes, I want to buy the widget from you" the mammalian part of his brain has to be silently communicating to him, "I feel good about the decision I'm making."

What positive emotions are you selling? In the selling process emotions are involved in two very distinct components. First, no matter what type of product or service you represent, you also represent the emotions that are attached to the item. People perceive and process experiences, new information and incoming data and immediately attach emotions to the experiences and information in order to remember them. When introduced to your product or service the customer recalls any similar situations or experiences that are related and filter your product through what they already know, understand and feel about what you're selling.

Do you know how your customer feels about purchasing what you're selling? Do you know the underlying feelings associated with your product or service? The vulnerability? The fear? The security? The joy? What perspective does the customer have about your product or service based on his prior experiences? Is his perspective generally negative or positive when it comes to filtering the new information you provide him on your products and services?

Second, emotions interplay between the people that are involved in the sale. Most of us commonly mistake this as; *I need to get my customer to like me. If the customer thinks I'm great then I increase my chances of closing the sale.* This is not entirely the case. Humans are more egocentric than we give them credit for in the above assumption. Instead of worrying so much about whether the potential customer likes you, focus on whether he feels comfortable and confident with himself when he is with you.

If the customer feels you are validating him, making him feel comfortable and confident, then he will like you because you positively reflect good feelings toward him. It is not about winning over the positive associations the customer has about you, the Seller, but making sure the customer feels good about himself, the Buyer. Building client rapport begins with making the customer feel confident about himself, not about proving your confidence levels to the customer. If you can validate the customer and make him feel good about himself, his liking you won't even be an issue.

These same emotion-based selling principles hold true when you're asking your boss for a raise, when you're "selling" your partner on the idea of sharing household duties, when you need your teenager to participate or when you ask others to volunteer their time and energy for a cause.

What solutions are you selling? As stated earlier, the person who wanted a drill needed a hole. The good salesperson at the local hardware store knows the solution to the underlying need of the customer. Most successful companies are very aware of what extended needs their products or services meet. For example, hospitals realize that staying in business goes beyond providing excellent medical services. They also need to take on the persona of being in the hotel business. They know the solutions to the underlying needs of excellent room service, reservations and providing acceptable accommodations. What are the underlying and extended needs involved with your product and how are you providing the solutions?

Are you asking the right questions to increase your selling profit? To find out what it is that you're "really" selling you need to ask the right questions. The right questions will help you identify your two key components. One, the emotion, and two, the solution to the underlying need.

There are four key interconnected areas in every customer's life: Personal, Work, Couple and Friends/Family. There are underlying needs and surface wants in each of these four areas. (Read Chapter Four.) Overlap each of these four areas with an emotional, physical, intellectual and spiritual layer and you technically have sixteen categories for identifying needs and wants for which you can provide solutions. Are you asking the right questions in order to successfully identify the areas in which you can provide good feelings and solutions?

Do your customers have aging parents? Do your customers lead an active lifestyle? Do they have children who want to attend college? Family inherited health risks? A partner to cherish and protect? A stressful job? A large family in which to provide presents for at every big occasion? A high profile job with numerous events that require multiple event resources or at the very least do they require a decent wardrobe? Do your customers operate in a hazardous work environment? A friendly work environment? The list goes on and on. Ask questions that show you are interested in and truly care about your customers' needs and wants so that you can provide the best, most customized solution to their specific underlying needs.

Follow up with questions that help the customer realize and experience the positive emotions associated with your product or service or request. What would the benefits be to the customer for having your product or service, for lending you and your cause a hand or for taking on more household duties? What would be the benefits to his children, or spouse, or colleagues or the marketing department? How might your product meet his identified cost reduction needs? How might you two build a seller-buyer relationship together that makes him feel comfortable? What does "the best fit" long term package look and feel like to him?

What's the bottom line on Neuro-Sales™ Techniques? First, ask your customers the right questions to find out the solutions they truly seek. Then provide your potential customers' brains with the solutions they crave to meet the underlying needs of their surface wants.

Second, give your potential customers' brains what they want: positive emotions to support the "logical" decision of purchasing your product or service. Positive emotions that directly affect the perception of your product. Positive emotions that elicit good feelings about the customers so they feel comfortable and confident about *themselves* and the decisions they make in your presence.

Chapter Seven
Ever have a stressful day?!

The kind of day when you're irritable and short on patience and your heart rate picks up speed, your blood pressure increases, your back is tense and your neck muscles tighten up so much that you're afraid if you move your head the wrong way the whole thing might snap off. The type of day where many of these symptoms are in full swing by ten am; leaving you with long hours to survive, meetings to endure and people to deal with.

Whether you are trying to juggle laundry, meals, board meetings, cleaning, children, aging parents, friendships, a career, a relationship with your spouse or significant other, an entire division of a company, physical exercise, car pools or volunteer responsibilities, your schedule leaves little time for paying attention to your stress levels.

Almost every day you deal with the pressures and demands of your job, your family and friends, your partner and yourself. You make choices all day long to help meet your needs and to help meet the needs of others. When your own needs and values get compromised, or when your needs and values come in conflict with the needs and values of others stress is created. How you manage and cope with the daily demands and pressures on your values and needs determines whether or not you are overly stressed, under stressed or optimally stressed.

Stress is inevitable, but you'll be surprised to know that it's actually needed. That doesn't stress you out does it?! It's when you mismanage it or when you don't manage it at all that it creates trouble. You can't function with too much stress in your life, and you can't function with too little stress. If some charlatan claims he can eliminate stress from your life, don't buy it. Literally. As crazy as it sounds, you need a certain amount of stress so that you can perform at your best. While too much stress can be mentally, emotionally and physically disruptive, not having enough stress can reduce your motivational resources and your energy levels. Finding the right amount of stress to achieve optimal levels of performance is no easy task, and your ideal stress level is unique to you.

Where does stress come from? From your emotional reaction to every event, every person, and every set of circumstances you encounter. You can get stress from work, from family and friends, from your partner and from yourself. Yes, you! Sometimes you can be your own worst enemy thinking about all the horrific things that will probably never happen to you, feeling guilty, way too guilty over small mistakes, hereafter referred to as learning opportunities, and pretty much just beating yourself up for not being perfect. Ugh. You'll never win the perfectionist race. So here and now, instead of pursuing perfection and always losing, start pursuing excellence and you'll discover you're a frequent winner.

One of the greatest stressors in life is change and your reaction to it. Whenever you transition from what you know and are comfortable with to the unknown, you emotionally and mentally have to adjust. Your ability to adjust to external events and change is based on your perception of how much control you have over what is happening around you and how accepting you are of that which is not in your control. Your ability to successfully adjust is also determined by how much value you place on being in control and the degree to which you must compromise or defend your needs.

Suppose your company is downsizing and many people are being laid off. If you are offered several options about your future and feel you have some control over the choice you make you will feel less stressed than if you feel you have no control over your future. Additionally, your perception of being laid off is influenced by the value you place on having some control over the choice you make and whether or not the options offered can still meet your needs. If you are a financially secure fifty seven year old, and were anticipating retirement before you knew of the downsizing, you will feel very differently about the various severance packages offered to you than the forty-two year old who has to support her two college aged children, and who feels that the options offered to her don't even come close to meeting her needs.

Depending upon your perception of events and circumstances and the perspective you take on these happenings, you will either produce high levels of stress related hormones, or you will produce low levels of stress related hormones. Therefore, stress technically comes from you. It is triggered by external events, but it is created in your brain. How you perceive and process external events, and what emotion you place on these external events determines your level of stress.

How does stress affect your mind and body? Place your feet flat on the floor. Let your shoulders drop (if your muscles aren't too tight to do so). Focus on your toes. Concentrate on your toes, and as you concentrate, start scrunching your toes up and rolling them under. Go on, do it. Scrunch them up super tight and keep them scrunched under until they start to cramp. Release. Relax. Question for you: Did you hold your breath while your toes were scrunched?

The majority of you did. You will focus so much on the strain that you forget to breathe. It's okay, it's normal, and the moment you relaxed your toes you started breathing again. What does this small example have to do with stress? Everything!

Your brain requires twenty percent of the oxygen of every breath you take in order to fully function. When your body is under stress, even toe scrunching stress, it reduces the amount of oxygen to your brain, therefore reducing your ability to maximize your mind. When under stress your performance levels drop. What used to be referred to as fluffy, the whole mind/body connection "thing," is now being taken seriously because we have scientific research backing it up.

Within seventy-two hours of a significantly stressful event or day, your body reacts. Physically manifesting a cold, a headache, muscle spasms, acne, whatever strikes your body's fancy, you get. The mammalian part of your brain controls your immune system, your biorhythms, your emotions and your memory. If you think of your immune system and your biorhythms as living in the same house as your emotions, it's easier to comprehend the connection. They talk to each other, they interact, and they *react* to one another.

Most people are unaware that many of the symptoms that they experience are stress related. Research suggests that over seventy percent of people's physical symptoms and ailments are stress related. A staggering statistic.

When you are experiencing stress your body undergoes physiological changes in blood pressure, pulse rate and respiration. Meaning, your heart beats faster, your breathing changes and you may get sweaty palms or feel butterflies in your stomach or you may just get a tight muscle. These changes are exactly why lie detector tests work so well.

When you are experiencing stress you also produce higher than needed levels of hormones. One particular hormone called cortisol can wreak havoc when too much of it is produced by your adrenal glands. Cortisol is needed by your body to perform a wide variety of functions from your liver working properly to managing your levels of moodiness. Yet, too much cortisol can increase your blood sugar, may suppress your sexual desires and can cause proteins in your body to breakdown faster than normal, which can lead to muscle atrophy and osteoporosis, especially in women. Even worse, high levels of cortisol increase your risk for heart disease, which happens to be the number one killer of women and men in America. Too much cortisol also reduces the capability of your immune system to fight infection and disease. Being overly stressed for prolonged periods of time is a one-way ticket to an early death. No increase in personal and professional profit here!

How can you create balance and reduce stress in regard to your daily schedule of activities? You can't. Creating balance in your activities is not possible. Quit wasting your time. When it comes to life activities there is no such thing as balance, only priorities. You may change your priorities as much as you want, but if you strive for balance you'll only add to your stress levels, not reduce them.

Balance *can* be found in many aspects of your life, as explained later in this chapter, but trying to implement the concept of balance in regard to what you physically do with your time is misleading and can be harmful to your own well being.

Successfully dealing with life's pressures, demands and hassles means appropriately responding and managing the tasks at hand in order of priority. If someone you know is sick, you do not say, "I'm sorry, but this is my time to relax and read a book. You'll have to wait." If a colleague comes to you and says, "We just got the Miller account, we need to increase production rates by fifteen percent." You do not reply, "It'll have to wait. I'm going to look at some land I'm thinking of buying." Good grief. You respond. You re-prioritize what you need to do and then you act.

If you are trying to balance all of the things in your life that demand your time and attention you'll never succeed. If you prioritize the items demanding your time and attention, and respond accordingly, you will accomplish a reduction in your stress levels.

How many people do you know, possibly even yourself, who experience guilt for not being with their family when they are at work, and who feel guilt for not being at work when they are with their family? Think these people are experiencing a bit of stress?!

How do you determine your priorities? First, take the time to identify your values and figure out what is important to you. Then, make choices based on these values. *This* is where balance does come into play. It is critical to know what you value and what your needs are so that you can align these values and needs with your choices. Only when your choices are directly aligned (or in balance) with your values can you prioritize properly. When you prioritize according to your values you will feel good about the choices you are making, thus reducing your stress levels.

Rate the following eleven items in order of importance to you today. Number one equals the most important or the most valued item today. Number eleven equals the least important or the least valued item today.

Friends	Career	Health
Family	Leisure/Hobbies	Faith
Partner	Freedom	Education
Philanthropy	Financial Security	

1.	7.
2.	8.
3.	9.
4.	10.
5.	11.
6.	

Was this an easy task? Probably not. Sure, it might have been easy to rate your first two or your last two but to place a ranked value system on everything in-between presumably created a bit of frustration for you. This is exactly why the exercise is needed and effective. You need to be fully aware of what you value in terms of "priority" rather than "importance" so you can make the right decisions regarding how you use your time every single day. No doubt, almost every item above is important to you, but do they all need to be a priority today? Perhaps not. Two weeks from now revisit this exercise. Your response may be quite different depending on the circumstances in which you find yourself. Absolutely okay. Shifting priorities is the only way to honor all of the things you value without the stress of trying to cram each and every item into each and every day.

What you value and choose to prioritize today is unique to you. Others may want to judge and criticize your actions, but their comments will only cause you stress and negative feelings if you have not taken the time to make sure that your choices directly align with your prioritized values.

What can you do to get the right level of stress for you and start increasing your personal and professional profit? Start making choices that reflect what you value and consider a priority to you today. What did you rate as number one today? Did you actually prioritize this value today or will you at least prioritize it in the next few days? If yes, great. If not, start re-prioritizing your time. What are your top six prioritized values? Do you spend higher percentages of your time shifting between these six priorities and successfully meeting these prioritized needs or are you trying to juggle and *balance* almost all of these items in your daily life?

Let go of the myth of balance in regard to how you spend your time. Each of the factors listed above will be a priority in turn and you can adjust your life accordingly to fulfill your needs. Sometimes your job will take priority. Sometimes your family will take priority. Sometimes you will take priority. Priorities shift and change. If you try to balance all of the items each and every day you will fail. If you focus on fulfilling your top three or six needs, when you successfully do meet them, you can then re-prioritize and focus on something else. It's either constant balance failure or constant priority fulfillment and it is constantly your choice.

When you reach the position of being able to respond to shifting priorities with an attitude of flexibility and acceptance rather than an attitude of frustration and helplessness you will know your optimal stress level.

What's the bottom line on reducing your stress?

1. Practice relaxation techniques that help restore normal levels of stress hormones in your body. Yoga, meditation and deep breathing can help.

2. Exercise. Exercising releases endorphins. Endorphins are your body's natural anti-depressant.

3. Talk positively to yourself. If you make a mistake, deal with it and move on. Quit worrying over the mistakes (aka: learning opportunities) you made yesterday, let alone five years ago. Start asking yourself what you learned from the incident, how it has made you a better person today and what choices

you can make today to keep moving in a healthy direction.

4. Learn to ask for help and say yes when it's offered. This is huge. Asking for help does not mean you are helpless. Asking for help means you are smart enough to realize that team work can get things done faster and better and leaves you with more time for your priorities.

5. Say please and thank you and mean it when you do say it. People will respond positively. Hint: Being appreciated and thanked meets a portion of your need for feeling valued and respected by others. If you sincerely appreciate and thank others, they'll be back to help even more.

6. Find a way to release tension that works for you and doesn't physically or emotionally harm you or others. Go to the gym, play a game or talk to a friend. Figure out what works best for you that still respects healthy choices and go for it.

7. Seek professional help. If you are experiencing prolonged periods of intense stress, find an expert to

help you reduce your stress. Your happiness and state of health depend on it.

8. Remember that stress is determined by your reaction to external circumstances and changes, and whether or not you feel in control of these happenings. Focus on the elements you can control and identify the extent to which you can minimize the negative impact on fulfilling your needs.

9. Quit searching for balance and start focusing on what it is you value today and how you can prioritize your activities around what you value.

Chapter Eight
Ever been on a diet?

Okay, okay, silly question, I'll wait until you're done laughing. For most of you the question isn't "Have you ever been on a diet?," but "When haven't you been on a diet?" With the media fixating on pencil thin curves, steel-python biceps, low fat-high fiber foods, getting your essential vitamins, blah, blah, blah, there are few of you who haven't dieted in some way shape or form. It's easy to see or not see the results of dieting on your body. The slacks fit, the slacks don't fit. But have you ever wondered what dieting does to your brain? Because you can't see the results of dieting on your mind you tend not to consider the consequences of food choices on your mental prowess.

Do you ever drink a cup of coffee or tea first thing in the morning? Do you ever eat toast, oatmeal or cereal for breakfast? While it certainly isn't illegal, it is the worst way to jumpstart your brain. Why? The brain like every other organ in your body is primarily made up of carbohydrates. However, there are three primary ingredients involved in optimal mental functioning.

These three key ingredients are fat, protein and water and your brain requires enormous amounts of each of them. When you wake up in the morning, your body is dehydrated. So is your brain. The best way to start the day is by re-hydrating your body and your brain by drinking eight ounces of water before you drink your daily cup of Joe. You will notice your energy level rise.

Carbohydrates are needed and necessary, but start your day with protein or a protein/carbohydrate combo. I'm a bread and bagel fan, but I savor the carbs after I've eaten protein or alongside some protein. Eggs, yogurt, cottage cheese, chicken, fish and soy all make for great breakfast diets. WHAT? Chicken for breakfast?

Ever eat leftovers for breakfast? I'm not talking about the crusty cold pizza from your college days, though pepperoni pizza is not a bad idea. I'm talking about great sources of protein for breakfast, the type we usually find at the dinner table but rarely find at the breakfast table. Marketing campaigns have told us we can find our essential vitamins and minerals in a cereal bowl, which is partially true, but the brain craves protein before it craves carbohydrates. Do you have to give up your cereal, toast and muffins? Absolutely not. In fact, as a self-admitting bread-aholic, banish the thought! Just add eggs, milk, chicken, fish, cheese, soy or whey proteins to your breakfast routine and your brain will thank you in intellectual ways.

Is your refrigerator full of low-fat, reduced-fat, and no-fat items? Watching your fat and cholesterol levels is certainly important. However, severely cutting fat from your diet has drastic results. Just as you are striving for peak physical performance, you need to strive for peak mental performance.

Medical research studies have proven that eliminating too much fat from your diet results in short term memory loss, a reduction in your ability to solve problems efficiently and accurately, decreased motivational levels and an overall decline in performance and productivity. Why? Your brain cells talk to each other via a substance called myelin. Myelin is a fatty secretion that allows the mind to make connections between the synaptic cells of the brain. Myelin coats the branches (axons) of all those neurons (tree trunks) in order to speed up the electrical impulses between cells. In other words, peak mental performance requires fat in your diet.

Example. You see a woman in the grocery store. You recognize her face, you recall that she is Linda from your accounting class. Without the assistance of fat, you can't recall her name or remember how you know her. Now, before you reach for those salty, greasy chips you adore, remember that the kind of fat your brain needs is not the type of saturated fat you find in junk food. It's the type of unsaturated fat you find in salmon, avocados and nuts.

How do you add fat and protein to your diet and stay healthy? Through balanced dietary changes, proportional amounts of the right kind of fats and consistent exercise. If you're watching your cholesterol, sausage and butter-laden pastries aren't great items to add to your breakfast plate, but soy sausages and cottage cheese (not low-fat) will provide your brain with the good fat it needs to start the day right. Fruit shakes with added protein provide the protein you need without the grease from fatty (saturated fat) foods.

So where does the fat you need come from if you eat soy protein sausage and drink smashed berries? From other, lower cholesterol sources that still contain the fat your brain craves and needs. These foods include, but are not limited to, yogurts (the full fat variety), milk, cottage cheese, nuts, avocado and fish such as salmon. Regular exercise is a necessary and needed component for both brain and body wellness. (For more information on the brain benefits of exercise read Chapters Seven and Ten.)

What do you need to eat for optimal brain function so you can increase your personal and professional profit?

1. Plenty of water throughout the day, most especially when you first wake up. Water keeps your brain and body hydrated and boosts your energy levels.

2. Tyrosine-rich protein found in such foods as yogurts, shellfish, dark turkey meat, salmon, tuna, beef, soy (tofu) and whey. Protein is the brain's essential fuel. (Note: approximately thirty percent of your daily caloric intake should come from protein.)

3. Fat. The "good for you" Omega-3 variety found in avocados, cheeses, meats, unhydrogenated oils and nuts. This will keep your cells firing, wiring and staying connected. (Note: approximately thirty percent of your daily caloric intake should come from fat.)

4. Vegetables and fruits, most especially dark, green leafy vegetables including broccoli, spinach and lettuce, and fruits such as strawberries, blueberries and kiwi. Vitamin C levels are higher in the brain than anywhere else in the body, in some cases as much as 15 times higher. Vitamin C blocks the effects of free radicals

whose key job is to reduce blood flow to the brain and impair memory. More importantly, Vitamin C is involved in the manufacturing of neurotransmitters, the substance required for communication between nerve cells. (Note: Too much Vitamin C may contribute to severe health problems such as kidney stones. All in balance.)

5. Iron found in lean red meat, fish, poultry and dried legumes. Iron carries oxygen to your brain via the bloodstream and allows for full mental functioning in your neocortex.

6. B vitamins found in eggs, pork and fish help regulate hormone levels and activate neural movement. Without B12, sourced in dairy products, you cannot store and retrieve memory, as it is a key player in creating the amino acid directly involved in protein synthesis, which creates the outer layer of neurons. A highly technical way of saying, no B12 - no brain function.

It's vital to get a proper balance of B vitamins, especially B6, as a deficiency of B6 limits cell response and too much B6 can create hyperactivity and increased blood flow which can actually impair focused thinking. The right amount of B6 though, is perfect for fighting age-related impairments in brain performance. (Note: If digesting B vitamins in pill form, take them in the morning as they have mild stimulant properties.)

7. Vitamin A found in milk products and eggs and Vitamin E found in spinach, nuts and corn oil are additional antioxidants (sort of like cousins to Vitamin C) that reduce the damage free- radicals can do to your nerve cells.

Your body and brain also need carbohydrates at the right time and in the right amount. Carbohydrates are the base and largest section of the food pyramid for a reason. Complex carbohydrates (such as whole grains or beans and rice) are best for the brain and can be added to any meal. Approximately forty percent of your daily caloric intake should come from carbohydrates.

An optimal time for pasta is dinner and it should be served in small portions. Why dinner? Eating excessive carbs at lunch will make you sleepy at four o'clock due to the release of insulin which lowers glucose levels. Eating couscous, pasta or rice at dinner will slow you down just in time for bed. Why small portions? Packing huge amounts of carbs into your body will result in added weight, unless you're a marathon runner. For the majority of us though, a smaller portion of carbs balances out the average amount of walks, biking and/or trips we take to the gym.

What's the bottom line on your brain diet? Give your brain what it wants: plenty of "good for you" fat, protein (especially at breakfast) and water. Lots and lots of water. Give your brain the fuel it needs so it can give you what you need: a great tool for dealing with the days ahead.

Chapter Nine
How do you deal with a "difficult" person?

Dealing with a "difficult" person has unfortunately become an almost daily activity. Some of you may even schedule a specific time in your day for dealing with the more "difficult" phone calls, meetings and interactions you have to perform. Some of you may just hope, wish and pray that if you do not return the "difficult" person's phone call they'll magically fall off of the planet and it will save you another seventeen minutes of aggravation, frustration and heartburn.

Conflict is everywhere. There is no escaping the many differences of opinion, various viewpoints, a wide range of wants and needs and people's inability to communicate in the process. With so many people having different goals, objectives and beliefs conflict is actually inevitable. So what do you do these days when conflict is occurring all around you, when your own stomach has betrayed you by developing a tolerance for the antacid tablets you pop like candy, and your colleagues, or clients or neighbors still insist on saying the opposite of everything you say?

You change. Yes, *you* change. When you find yourself in conflict it is because *you* cannot get what you want or what you need and/or because *you* have chosen to act a certain way. By changing what you want, what you need or your actions you change the outcome of conflict. This change in you is not about altering your fundamental core values and beliefs. It is about changing how you interact with the "difficult" person in order to create the ideal outcome for you.

What is conflict? Conflict is frequently described as opposing views, opposite wants or needs, arguments, struggles, fighting, dealing with jerks and/or participating in situations involving disagreement and sometimes volatile emotions.

However, conflict can also be defined as an opportunity to discover new insights; as inevitable, normal and needed; or as a precursor to creativity and invention. With these two radically different viewpoints on the definition of conflict a debate could very well occur, but conflict, whether seen as positive or negative is simply defined by perspective.

Where does conflict reside? You might be tempted to say conflict resides in the "difficult" person's mouth every time he or she opens it, but conflict actually resides in *your* brain. Conflict is emotional. The emotional reaction within your brain is triggered by the perceived or actual threat of losing something important to you. This perception of loss creates conflict. If you perceive to be losing dignity, time, control, or something of value your brain triggers an emotional response.

How does conflict occur within the brain? In the human brain you have two oval structures in the limbic region known as amygdalas. Your amygdalas serve as the control center of your emotional mind. Each amygdala scans all incoming information sent to it from the thalamus and assesses its value. (The thalamus is a structure in your brain that serves as a translator; essentially decoding all incoming data into a language that the brain can understand.) The amygdala will assign each piece of decoded data an emotional value. For instance, it is your thalamus that recognizes an elderly neighbor when you open the door, but it is the amygdala that informs you how fond you are of her because she reminds you of your own sweet grandmother. Depending upon the intensity of the emotion assigned, the amygdala will either send the emotional data directly to your

113

neocortex for further processing, or the amygdala will take over and send signals throughout the brain calling for immediate action and emergency responses.

If the amygdala tells the rest of the brain that the current situation needs a survival response it will emit emergency signals that cause the neocortex to "shut down" long enough for other parts of the brain to dominate and keep you alive. This reaction allows for a strong "fight or flight" response which ensures survival. Once the threat has passed, the amygdala calms down, stops overproducing hormones, and allows the neocortex to fully function again. Even if the situation is not dangerous enough to warrant an instinctive survival response, the amygdala can still overreact and assign an emotional value that causes your neocortex to shut down and your body to be flooded with hormones.

Example. Suppose an individual, named Thalamus, serves as host at a quaint restaurant. Thalamus watches everything going on in the restaurant and processes all happenings to ensure the successful operations of the restaurant. Amygdala, the owner, regularly receives updates from Thalamus, and is also very aware of auditory and visual cues and can even smell the various entrees, the wine selections and the distinct colognes of each patron. Amygdala scrutinizes every sensory experience to make sure life is acceptable and good in the restaurant.

A couple arrives for dinner. They confirm their seven o'clock reservation. Thalamus welcomes them and seats them and informs them that their waiter, Hippocampus will be with them shortly. (Hippocampus is the structure in your brain responsible for a huge number of things including the memory of dry facts.) Thalamus then informs Amygdala and Hippocampus that table seventeen has been filled. On and on this pattern of welcoming guests, seating them, serving them and thanking them for coming runs smoothly until the dreaded, Mr. and Mrs. Difficult arrive.

Upon seeing the couple, Thalamus informs Amygdala and Hippocampus of the couples' presence and continues with routine behavior. Amygdala, however, upon recognizing that these two people serve as restaurant critics for a huge national newspaper and are known for their caustic reviews, immediately starts flooding the restaurant with hormones. Amygdala, who is causing a rush of adrenaline, anxiously starts firing rapid commands at the chef, knowing from prior experience how the entire evening is likely to turn out. These instantaneous commands are shouted without Amygdala taking the time to consult with Neo Cortex, the restaurant manager, for perhaps a better plan of response.

Amygdala proclaims "crisis" throughout the restaurant and beckons all staff to now pay attention to helping everyone survive the visit. Hippocampus walks over to the couple and starts rattling off the various specials of the evening, only to discover that Mr. and Mrs. Difficult don't like anything being offered. They would rather have something unique created. Hippocampus relates this fact to Amygdala who panics even more, who seems to be on the verge of tears, and who then starts babbling about the possibility of the couple writing a bad restaurant review, thus causing the restaurant to go under and make everyone homeless.

When every person on staff receives the message that this couple could ruin their future and make them homeless, they panic and expend tremendous amounts of energy making sure everything is satisfactory for the couple. The majority of the night goes well, with only a few crazy phrases uttered from nervous mouths, but finally, the couple pays and gets ready to head out the door. Everyone breathes a sigh of relief as they hear Mrs. Difficult tell Thalamus they had a wonderful meal.

Just then, Neo Cortex happens to walk out from the back office. Neo thanks the couple for their patronage and actually invites them back again! Amygdala, having calmed down now that the threat of losing the restaurant is over, approaches Neo and tells Neo what happened. Neo analyzes the situation and tells Amygdala that the reaction was too dramatic and that Neo should not have been shut out from helping. Amygdala feels defensive and explains that duty for survival called. It was important to the very existence of the restaurant that all go well. Neo listens to Amygdala and respects the emotions Amygdala has just gone through. Neo takes all these emotions into consideration and tells everyone that since this is so important to Amygdala, and since the couple may very well be back, Neo will devise a plan for future visits, and reminds Amygdala that the plan will work, but only if Amygdala informs Neo of the couple's arrival.

Your emotional mind is directly involved in situations where you have to deal with a "difficult" person. Just as in the scenario above, your amygdala can overreact and take over your brain thus shutting out your neocortex. However, unlike the drawn out example above, research has proven that it takes approximately five to seven seconds for your amygdala to receive the data, assign an emotional value to it and then pass the emotion along to the neocortex or commandeer your whole brain in order to get you into survival mode. Five to seven seconds!

What if the amygdala overreacts in a non-survival situation? When you make a big deal about a minor incident, or you become melodramatic or excessive in your reaction, your amygdala has labeled the incoming data as highly volatile and you react without "thinking." Something about the incoming data, based on past experiences, triggers an intense emotional response and your amygdala shuts down the neocortex so your brain can pay full attention to the over escalated emotion. Ever put your foot in your mouth? Ever respond to someone a bit melodramatically? Have you ever been a tad "hot under the collar" to only feel like a fool later on in the day? You're not alone. Everybody has experienced an amygdala invasion of the brain at some point in his or her life.

Why do you sometimes over-react to "difficult" people? Your emotional circuits are primarily developed by age four. How you handled early experiences, how adults around you behaved in emotional situations and the genes you were given all influence your skills for dealing with emotions. Does this mean you can't rewire your reactions? No, you can change your neural pathways; it just takes conscious choice to do so and some great tools.

Every situation that occurs for you today is compared to every similar situation you have already experienced. Once the current experience is linked to a comparable past experience, your emotional mind will create a similar response in feelings. For instance, think of a person that irritates you. Every time you encounter this person you quickly compare it to all the times you have previously interacted with him or her. Upon visual recognition you instantly groan and start to feel irritated. You feel irritated before s/he has even said or done anything because your emotional mind instantaneously recalls all past experiences and feelings associated with this individual. If this person has ever actually been nasty to you, your heart might even race a bit at the thought of another confrontation. Suppose though, that today, this same person smiles and tells you to have a great day, and then keeps walking. What is your mental thought? *Hey, they might actually be decent.* No way. Your mind immediately thinks - *Jerk!* Even though current circumstances should dictate that we mentally think, *nice person*, there is no way your perception filters are going to radically shift away from every prior experience you have had with this individual. The neural circuitry for associating the person's face with the emotional value of *Jerk!* is too strong for instant rewiring.

The same principle works in reverse. If someone you love and think is terrific is a royal pain in the derriere one day, you do not immediately think of him as a jerk. Rather, you assume he is having a rough day, and so you supply a hug or a few words of encouragement and move on yourself. No big deal to you.

In order to decrease conflict and increase your "no big deal to me" reactions to others, you need tools for creating new neural pathways. New pathways can help you change your own habitual reactions and your own behaviors. These new neural pathways will help you improve the way you deal with a "difficult" person by helping you to react to present circumstances and not prior experiences.

What can you do to better deal with a "difficult" person and increase your personal and professional profit since you can't put the "difficult" person in a headlock and give him a noogie?

1. Start with remembering the ten second rule. Why ten? If on average it takes five to seven seconds for your amygdala to take charge within your brain, then by allowing a few more seconds, you increase the likelihood of your brain's hormonal levels equalizing out again. Count to ten, slowly. It's actually an incredibly long amount of time when you're trying not to respond to a "difficult" person. However, by waiting to react, you give your neocortex an opportunity to enter the picture and help you analyze a better choice of action. This means less foots inserted, less faux pas, reduced volatility, better consequences and perhaps even less regrets.

2. Change the environment when possible. In many cases, you do not have to deal with a "difficult" person in the moment of conflict. You tend to think that you have to react instantaneously in order to be heard or to get your point across. However, you actually increase your ability to deal effectively with the person if you wait until your emotional response is diluted. Most conflict occurs with people you know. Not all, but most. This provides you with an opportunity to wait and reschedule a meeting or discussion with this person at a later date and possibly a better place. A different time of day, another day entirely or a less territorial venue (without other people watching) can help you better handle the conflict.

Distancing yourself from the conflict provides your brain with an opportunity to problem solve, process, make connections and come up with a solution or tactic that is more appropriate and fitting than it would have created otherwise. Stepping away from the "difficult" person also reduces the emotional energy you feed them. Typically, if they see they're getting a rise out of you and causing you to get "hot under the collar" it just adds fuel to their own tactics and provides them with an added advantage.

3. Choose your words carefully. Often times you may think you're reducing tension, when in fact you're actually helping to build it. You may think you are being helpful, when in actuality you are invalidating the other person's feelings. Remember, conflict resides in your emotional mind when the threat of loss is triggered. Even though you may disagree with a person's actions, you still need to validate their feelings.

Sometime in your life you were probably told not to feel the way you did, or you were told to actually stop feeling what you were at the time, or you might have been told to toughen up because you were being too sensitive. Being ignored, judged or told that your feelings are wrong invalidates you, and this will make you angry and defensive because your feelings are a huge part of you.

When dealing with a "difficult" person who is clearly upset, if you tell them to "stay calm" you will only incite increased hostility because they cannot possibly "stay calm" when their amygdala is in commandeer mode. The best thing to do is state an emotion you think they are feeling. The single utterance of an emotion they might be feeling instantly validates what they are experiencing and tells them that you "get it."

Suppose an individual you know is ranting and raving about the ineptitude of colleagues, the inefficiencies of the systems that are in place and is pretty much venting at top speed. Telling him that he should get over it, that it's just the way it works, will only incite more ranting, with no focus toward a solution. Conversely, if you respond when he takes a breath, with the word, *"frustrating,"* or with the phrase, *"that's really frustrating,"* this individual is going to look at you and say, *"You're darn right it's frustrating....blah, blah, blah."* More venting may occur, but then the individual will either thank you for listening or he will leave with the thought that he was heard.

Even if the emotion you state is slightly off the mark, the person will still feel validated. If you had said *"upsetting"* instead of *"frustrating"* in the scenario above, the individual might have said, "N*ot really, it's more frustrating than anything.*" No matter, at least he knows you're listening and you are accepting of how he feels because you're trying to identify his emotion.

Phrases or words that seek to identify a person's emotions can quickly deflate the energy and intensity behind the emotion. Questions can also be fantastic for deflating conflict. *Can I help in any way? What can I do to support you? Can we do anything to resolve this situation? How do you think we should resolve this scenario?* are all great questions for discovering if the person just wants to vent or if they are really looking for a solution to the problem.

4. Reframe the situation. Rarely is conflict ever about what it seems to be about on the surface. Rarely is the conflict about you. People process and perceive other people and events based on their own prior experiences. Prior experiences that may have nothing to do with you. A "difficult" person's actions or comments usually come about from an intent that is good, even though the approach may be challenging. Very few people wake up in the morning, stretch and say, "I can't wait to make so and so's life miserable today." Distancing yourself by reframing the "difficult" person as someone seeking their own underlying needs increases your recognition that they, just like you, are trying to figure it all out.

5. Listen. Listen so you may truly value their perspective and not so you can just answer back. If you listen for an underlying need that is not being met for them and if you listen for what they believe they are losing, you will ask better questions, respond with more validating remarks and decrease the overall tension.

6. Avoid entering into conflict with the idea that you are going to change the "difficult" person. Only you can change *your* reaction, your approach, *your* comments, *your* behaviors. Trying to change someone else is like beating your head against a brick wall, it feels good when you stop.

7. Change what you want or need. Assess what your own position is and why the conflict is occurring. What are your feelings and why are you feeling what you do? What are you essentially losing? What underlying need is not being met for you? What is the value of this want/need/loss to you? Can you let it go? Can you compromise? Can you get this want or need met elsewhere? Is getting it met elsewhere acceptable and appropriate to those involved in the conflict? Is the outcome of this conflict going to impact your future positively, negatively or not very much at all?

8. Remember your rights. You too have the right to be listened to, to be validated and to be respected. If the "difficult" person cannot accept that resolving conflict is a two-way street, then walk away. It's your right to politely inform them of your rights and to request that your rights be respected. Sometimes no matter how understanding you might be, some people may be so "difficult" that you actually need to choose to not waste any more of your time on them than is absolutely necessary.

What's the bottom line on dealing with a "difficult" person? How well you deal with a "difficult" person is entirely up to you. It is highly unlikely to change somebody else's "difficult" behavior, but you can change your own needs and wants, your own behaviors and your own perspective.

Chapter Ten
My aging brain?!

You're not getting any younger, nor is your brain, but that isn't exactly surprising news. What is surprising is that getting older isn't as bad as you might think, and the fountain of "brain youth" may be more in your grasp than you ever thought possible. In fact, as more and more research studies are conducted, scientists and doctors are discovering that your brain is quite flexible and adaptable up until you take your very last breath.

While long-term memory may be less dependable as you grow older, your ability to communicate, think abstractly, solve problems and make good decisions remains steadfast throughout your lifetime. As you age your brain will lose some power and speed, but it will also begin to utilize more parts of itself in order to compensate for a slower processing rate. Similar to a computer when it has run out of RAM, your brain isn't just slowing down because you're physically old, but rather it has accumulated so much information over the years that it requires some extra time to connect all of the cells that will contribute to the formulation of a wise answer.

There is a catch or string attached. You must use your brain well and often in your earlier years if you want to use it well and often in your later years. The old cliché, "use it or lose it" really does apply to your aging brain.

How does your brain evolve as you grow older?
Not the way all brain myths would have you believe.

Myth #1
One of the biggest myths about the aging brain is that every day you lose brain cells that are integral to your ability to mentally function. Not true. While your brain does reach its peak size in your early twenties, you do not stop learning and maturing at age twenty (I would hope). Your brain may indeed be at it's biggest when you're younger, but bigger doesn't necessarily mean better. Your brain, as it matures, actually sheds only those cells that are not contributing to your mental faculties. It sheds approximately one hundred thousand nonessential cells per day in order to make room for brand new dendrite and axonal connections that help you grow wiser. You may flinch at this number, but remember, you have billions of cells with over forty quadrillion possible

connections. Losing a hundred thousand cells per day is like your favorite beach losing a single grain of sand. Feel better now?

Myth #2
Once you reach your twenties, your brain stops growing and you're stuck with what you've got. Not true. Neurogenesis, the creation of nerve cells, allows the older brain to rebuild weakened structures so that the brain can grow old gracefully.

Compare the aging brain to the idea of buying a house. You enjoy looking at a brand new house because everything works, everything is fresh and there are no cracks or wrinkles in the foundation or roof - yet. The drawback to a lot of the new houses is that they are all pretty much the same and lack personality. On the other hand, when you walk into a house that's sixty or seventy years old, the plumbing may not be in great shape, but what character and charm it radiates. The older houses bubble over with such great stories and quirks that they make the younger houses seem dull and boring. With a bit of "restoration" things can work almost as good as new, you may just need a little more patience with the fact that everything isn't perfect.

Your brain will naturally restore itself if chemicals, drugs or any other physically traumatic incidents haven't harmed it. It will adapt, change and restore so long as you give it the tools it needs.

Myth #3
You automatically start losing your "marbles" as you age. Not necessarily true. Your brain does age, but loss of memory and your reduced ability to concentrate may have far more to do with what you did in your twenties and thirties than the fact that you're in your sixties or seventies now. Your loss in mental functioning or increase in mental functioning as you get older is partially influenced by the preceding years of behavioral choices. What you do today influences how your brain will perform one year from now and ten years from now. Make brain brilliant choices today and you radically increase your odds of being brain brilliant in your eighties, nineties and beyond.

The more stimulated your brain, the more dendrite – axon connections you make, therefore, the more connections your brain can rely on to function properly. However, if you aren't going to bother to use your brain cells, your own brain won't bother to keep them for you. It's normal to lose approximately ten percent of your brain cells over a lifetime. It's the prevention of a greater loss than this ten percent that you can control by your daily choices.

How do you start increasing your personal and professional profit right now so that you are brain brilliant as you grow older? If you are seven, twenty-seven, eighty-seven, or any age in-between, you can apply the following suggestions and get an incredible return on your investment.

1. Get moving! Exercise stimulates cell activity in the brain and can improve memory. The higher your heart rate, the more oxygen you get into your body and your brain. As you get older your reaction times decrease more from lack of fitness than from lack of youth. Walking and weightlifting are fantastic for body and brain fitness.

2. Get mental exercise. Read, take a class on a new subject or interest, play board games with others, solve mental puzzles, paint, complete a jigsaw puzzle, start a book club, visit a museum. Essentially, get out of your ruts and provide your brain with new opportunities to be challenged. When you learn something new, no matter the subject, you change the structure of your brain. The more you mentally exercise your brain in your younger

years the more likely you are to prevent or at least delay cognitive diseases decades later.

3. Eat right. Talk to your doctor about a diet plan that works for you. Whether you're twenty-five or seventy-five, big-boned or small-boned, short or tall, you need a diet that properly fuels your specific body type and your brain. There are fundamental components to a brain-based diet (Read Chapter Eight), but the diet you need at seventeen differs from the diet you need at fifty-seven and it's vitally important to give your brain and body proper nutrition.

4. Volunteer. Interact with others, talk with others, and give to others. Stay actively involved. Stimulate your mind and heart through active participation in an area of your choice. If you don't like to hammer, then read to those who are ill, if you don't want to read to others then help raise funds. It doesn't matter how you serve, just get involved in a cause or need outside of yourself. It will energize you, motivate you, get you actively participating in life and it'll keep those brain cells firing and wiring with a purpose.

5. Quit smoking. Now. Smoking limits the amount of oxygen fed to your brain and increases your potential for

Alzheimer's. If you need support to quit smoking, get it. There's no disgrace in asking for help, especially when the goal is to live a longer, healthier, brain brilliant life.

6. Avoid excessive consumption of alcohol. Alcohol does not melodramatically destroy brain cells, that's another myth, but it does keep your dendrites from communicating properly. With enough repeated exposure to large quantities of alcohol and the subsequent withdrawal phase afterwards, you can cause damage to brain cell activity.

7. Realize that as you get older you may need to slow down, but it doesn't mean you have to stop. Getting fit and staying fit applies to your mental and physical success and the two are totally intertwined. If you are slowing down, accept it and do what you can. Just keep moving and focus on how brain brilliant you can still be.

8. Reduce your stress levels. (Read Chapter Seven.)

9. Hug someone or some animal. No doubt you have heard countless suggestions that seniors should have pets. They should and so should you, especially if you live alone. When you hug another human being or stroke a friendly pet your body produces a hormone called

oxytocin. Oxytocin serves many purposes in the body, but when it is produced as a result of touching, it helps you feel relaxed, less stressed and more positive. (Pets are great at any age.)

10. Travel. It doesn't matter whether you visit a place that is thirty, three hundred or three thousand miles from home, just go visit and explore. New routines, new tastes, new sights and new sounds help your brain develop new dendrite-axon connections. These connections increase your brain density. If "getting around" is difficult for you, and/or traveling makes you nervous, join a group, or travel with family or friends and do your homework regarding safety. Your brain craves the new, exciting and different so stimulate it with travel and not only will you be brain brilliant you may make some new friends in the process.

11. Take time to discover your own interests and talents. Then pursue your talents with passion and delight. Having an outlet for your talents and gifts keeps you mentally and physically fit and increases self-esteem, which then makes you want to be even more mentally and physically fit. It's a healthy cycle.

If you implement all eleven factors above can you completely avoid age related ailments to the brain? Completely avoid? No. Possibly prevent or at the very least delay or reduce your symptoms? Yes. Growing older isn't always easy on the brain. There are many diseases that cause dementia; the most notable these days include but are not limited to Alzheimer's, Parkinson's, Huntington's, Multiple Sclerosis, and Lou Gehrig's.

Some brain diseases show up early in life, some diseases begin their onset in your teens or in mid-life, but the majority of dementia cases are reported by seniors, especially in the case of Alzheimer's. Dementia affects more than forty percent of Americans over eighty. At least one person in four over the age of eighty-five is diagnosed with Alzheimer's.

What is Alzheimer's? What is dementia? Are they the same thing? How do you get them? Alzheimer's is the name of a disease that creates dementia. Alzheimer's is a brain disorder in which nerve cells in the brain die. Picture a fork with tines. The fork represents the branches on each nerve cell. When the tines have food stuck between them it's difficult for the fork (cell) to function. If you can keep the tines clear between every bite it tends to work better. Alzheimer's likes to plug up the area

135

between the tines of the fork (the area between your brain cell branches) with a substance called plaque. A brain inflicted with Alzheimer's gets tired of a fork that doesn't work, and essentially throws the fork out. When the fork is thrown out (essentially meaning your nerve cells die off) communication inside the brain breaks down. A person with Alzheimer's disease then develops impairments to memory and fundamental brain function called dementia.

The exact cause of Alzheimer's is not known, though doctors and researchers suspect an interplay of genetic and environmental influences. Researchers have found evidence of a link between Alzheimer's and genes on three chromosomes, but they still have not figured out why some people with the gene and some people without the gene still get it. A tremendous amount of research still needs to be conducted, especially with the percentage of people inflicted with Alzheimer's (Baby Boomers) steadily increasing.

Dementia is a byproduct of disease, but is not a disease in and of itself. Dementia is the group of symptoms caused by various diseases or conditions that directly reduce your brain's ability to perform properly. Dementia develops when certain cells of the brain (those cells responsible for learning, memory, decision-making, and/or language) are affected by an infection or a disease and die off. Symptoms of dementia may include loss of mental functions such as thinking, memory, interpretation and analysis. These symptoms are severe enough to interfere with a person's daily life. Symptoms can also include changes in personality, mood swings and surprising behavior.

Dementia can be treated when it is caused by drugs or alcohol, or when hormone or vitamin levels are off kilter, but it cannot currently be treated if it is created by disease, which is why it is so important that you do everything you can today to prevent or delay its onset.

What's the bottom line on protecting your aging brain? Use it, use it early, keep using it and use it often. Participate fully in life, interact with others, get involved, stay mentally busy, stay physically active, eat right, reduce your stress levels, and be a life long learner. Your brain depends on an active mind.

Chapter Eleven
Ever been on a date?

For some this question produces smiles, giggles and fond memories. For others, this question produces nausea and hives. For clarity, I'm not referring to the type of date where halfway into the appetizer you wish you'd agreed to just meet for a drink rather an eight course meal. Rather, I'm referring to the kind of date that includes an attentive yet unobtrusive waiter, an inviting atmosphere and an entrée that transports you to another country's palette. The type of date where you have so much in common and so many exciting stories to share that the conversation effortlessly flows. The type of date where you can be yourself and you're accepted. The type of date where you are mentally stimulated, you laugh, you never say anything stupid and you feel like you are at your very best. Ever been on one of these types of dates? No? Well then it's time to have one! You deserve it. If yes, as a matter of fact, just last night, then congratulations.

However, the next date you have is going to be radically different than most of the other dates you've experienced. It's radically different because unlike your other dates where you actually went out with another person, the only company you are allowed this time is the camaraderie of the proverbial threesome "me, myself and I." That's right, I want you to have a date with yourself.

If you are married you do still in fact "date." You just happen to be married to your date. Great! However, you still need to go it alone every now and then, even if it means figuring out the calendar and scheduling a time to make it happen.

Why should you date yourself? As you made your way through this book you probably highlighted or underlined ideas you came across that were relevant to you. You might have even scribbled notes in the margins. In spite of these markings, after you finish reading this book, many of you will place it back in your bag, or on a shelf, or you will start a new pile somewhere in your home or office and this book will serve as a conduit for dust. You will toss this book somewhere because you are incredibly busy, and once you close the cover your life of action and activity will resume. A few months from now you might spy it, blow off the dust and think, "Oh yea, here's that book on the brain. It had some great ideas for improving my life." As the telephone rings you set it down and let it collect dust for another three months. It is exactly this "life of activity" that causes me to request that you schedule a date with yourself.

There is a well-known maxim that has been credited to a gentleman named Arthur Lenehan. He stated that, "After all is said and done, more is said, than done." He is sadly correct. Many of you will read this book, retain one percent, and continue with life as usual. Your one percent might have you start drinking more water, or asking more questions. Your one percent might have you using memory techniques so others more readily remember you or it might have you interviewing with a twenty-minute cycle approach. Perhaps you'll eat more protein, or analyze your underlying needs and create a Clear Cognitive Connection, but very few of you will implement all of the techniques described in this book in order to become phenomenally Brain Brilliant. Why? For the mere reason that it involves time, energy and diligence.

How can becoming Brain Brilliant be fun? By scheduling a date with yourself you significantly increase your likelihood of becoming Brain Brilliant. Whether this date means treating yourself to a great dinner, or taking yourself out to a beautiful park, or sitting down in your favorite chair or hiking your favorite hills, you need to do it. No matter the venue of choice, the goal is to take the time you need to revisit what you highlighted and underlined.

Schedule a date so that you may reread your scribbles in the margins and ask yourself what your needs, goals and objectives are for the next few weeks. Spend time reflecting and evaluating how the ideas in this book can revolutionize your life. What do you really need? What do you visualize for yourself three weeks from now, three months from now, three years from now? What about your life causes you great frustration? What brings you great joy? What can you do to reduce the frustrations and increase the joys? What resources do you need? Who can you talk to? What positive, forward-focused steps can you take to getting your life re-aligned with your values? Do you need to exercise your brain? Do you need to exercise your body? Do you need to modify your diet? What actions can you take to deal more effectively with conflict? What methods are you using to help you manage your stress levels? What else can you do to become even more Brain Brilliant?

Reflection and evaluation are the two highest levels of thinking you can do, but it is very difficult to reflect if you are constantly on the go. Make a date with yourself and review the ideas presented in this book. Create your personal action plan for becoming Brain Brilliant and then take the time to "date" yourself so you may check in with yourself on your progress with the plan.

Once you've started dating yourself again, then find others who are seeking Brain Brilliance. Form Brain Brilliant groups with others who want to engage in stimulating discussions, who want to travel to new places, who want to read new books and explore new hobbies. No, I do not mean form group therapy sessions, I mean form groups with others who share your excitement for growing a great brain. It is highly beneficial for you to receive positive support and encouragement from others as well as to feel accountable to others. Get your Brain Brilliant friends, colleagues, neighbors, or interest groups together several times a year or even monthly for a "Be Brain Brilliant" meeting.

It is always amazing to me that a few hours of reflective, analytical thinking can affect years of your life. It is truly the best gift you can give yourself. While it is understandable that you have many priorities and tasks that need your attention, and while it is understandable that people and situations seem to miraculously appear before you demanding your time and attention, it is still vital that you serve yourself first in order to better serve others. Take the time to "date" yourself so that you may put your Brain Brilliant ideas into action.

You have an opportunity to change your life and the lives of others for the better. The short amount of time it takes to reflect on your own Brain Brilliant journey will provide hours of new mental energies, more positive feelings, and a better chance of experiencing a more healthy and happy state of mind. It's your choice, your brain, and your opportunity to increase your personal and professional profit.

What's the bottom line on dating? Take action. Start with "dating" yourself. Reflect upon your own Brain Brilliant journey. Then "date" your partner or spouse and talk about what it is each of you is working toward and how you can support one another in becoming Brain Brilliant. Go out on group "dates" and create a forum for providing encouragement and accountability so all of you may be Brain Brilliant.

Dear Reader,

By now your mind is racing and buzzing. Excellent. That is the intention of this book; to serve as a catalyst in helping you capitalize on your own intelligence, your own education, your own experiences and your own self knowledge so that you may begin to maximize your brain in order to increase your profit both personally and professionally.

I have written this book not as an expert in neurology, nor as an expert in psychology, or even as an expert in biology. I have written this book as an expert in pedagogy. Teaching and learning.

Professionally, my undergraduate degree is in education from the University of Maryland, and my masters degree is in gifted education from Johns Hopkins University where I studied education with a specific emphasis on the role the brain plays in perceiving, processing, learning and behaving.

Personally, I am a life long learner with an avid interest in the brain and behavior. I seek out new information constantly, and can frequently be found with my face buried between a tome of encrypted pages, which verifies the nerdy but lovable reputation I have among family and friends. Learning for me is a passion that has only blossomed with age.

There is a tremendous amount of incredible, amazing, wondrous and life-changing knowledge to be learned, and it needs to be shared, in a way that is meaningful and applicable to all of us. Thus this book.

Brain Brilliant, Increase Your Personal and Professional Profit evolved from years of research, years of experience and years of mistakes. I find it easier to view these mistakes as learning opportunities, which is in the end, exactly what they were and are, but missteps nonetheless.

I have lived on carbohydrates for breakfast and wondered why I was irritable and lethargic at ten am; I have bossed others rather than asked; I have closed complex deals and yet struggled with simple sales; I have repeated behaviors I swore I'd never emulate; I have left goals unanswered and unfulfilled; have undergone incredible amounts of stress without tools to help me manage it; have tried remembering grocery items in my head only to return from the store sans much needed deodorant; have made completely logical, rational decisions that left me feeling intuitively upside down; have searched for fulfillment in ridiculous places and have learned an incredible amount in the process.

When the link between successful behavioral changes and an increased understanding of how my own mind fired and wired kept repeating itself, it became quite clear that the most remarkable and beneficial self-help tool I could ever acquire would be a better understanding of my own brain and the brains of others.

One of my favorite sayings is by Maya Angelou, and so I quote, "When we know better, we do better."

Knowing better is a life long journey and each new experience and opportunity provides valuable insights in helping us to evolve and do better.

There is never one complete tool kit to purchase in order to satisfy and meet all of our needs and teach us all of life's lessons. However, there are great tools, from many sources, that can be placed in your tool kit to help you achieve the potential and greatness that resides within you. Your brain and a better understanding of how it functions is one of these tools.

The origins of pedagogy come from the Greek paidagogia, from paidagogos, a slave who took children to and from school. In many ways this book is that servant, taking us all to the school of the brain and serving as the bridge that connects academia and science with our every day lives. Providing us all with an opportunity to "know better" so that we may "do better."

May this book be a servant that serves you well.

Respectfully,

AmyK

What would be the benefit
of sharing *Brain Brilliant* with others?

To order individual copies of the book visit www.AmyKInternational.com or Amazon.com. You can also fax this order form to 404.705.8545 or mail this order form to:

AmyK International, Inc.
Sales Department
PO Box 421276
Atlanta, Georgia, 30342

Looking for the perfect corporate gift? *Brain Brilliant* is *the* book to help you raise performance and productivity levels and increase your profitability.

Take advantage of our large order discounts.

If you are seeking to purchase a large quantity of books for a group, organization or company, please contact us directly at 404.705.8541 or email us at OurTeam@AmyKInternational.com.

Mr.❑ **Ms.**❑ **Mrs.**❑ **Dr.**❑				**First Name:**	
				Last Name:	

Title:
Company:
Personal or Business Address: Street Line 1
Street Line 2
Suite/Apt #

City	**State**	**Postal**
Code		

Telephone:	**Alternate Phone:**
Fax:	**Email:**
Website:	

AmyK® International accepts American Express, Visa, MasterCard and Discover. We also accept corporate checks. Please make checks payable to AmyK International.	Number of Copies: _____ Price per Book: _____ Handling Per Shipment: ____$2.95____ Shipping Per Book: $1.45 x # of books **Total Purchase:** _____
Name on Card: _____ **Cardholder Signature:** _____ By signing the above, you authorize AmyK International to charge your credit card the correct fee for the number of books purchased & shipped and any sales tax incurred.	Charge my: ❑American Express ❑Visa ❑MasterCard ❑Discover **Card Number:** _____ **3 Digit Number on Back of Card:** _____ **Expiration Date:** _____

Brain Brilliant™
Products and Services

AmyK® International provides workshops, training programs and presentations around the globe on Brain-Based Leadership Skills and Neuro-Sales™ Techniques. Through the innovative and effective combination of current scientific research, advanced adult education methodology and sound business development practices, AmyK introduces participants to how their minds work, how the minds of others work and the amazing benefit this information has on performance and productivity. Every perception, thought, feeling, decision and action has its own neural circuitry. Through the understanding of how our minds work and how the minds of others work, we can literally change our neural circuitry and change our behaviors. For more information on training programs, keynote addresses and the *Brain Brilliant* book series, please visit our website or please contact us at:

AmyK International
P.O. Box 421276
Atlanta, Georgia 30342

Telephone   404.705.8541
Fax   404.705.8545
Email   OurTeam@AmyKInternational.com
Website   www.AmyKInternational.com